D1242224

HOWEVER FAR THE STREAM FLOWS

PLATFORM

PRESS

BUCKS COUNTY
PENNSYLVANIA

HOWEVER FAR THE STREAM FLOWS

THE MAKING OF THE MAN WHO REBUILDS FACES

KOFI BOAHENE, M.D.

However Far The Stream Flows:
The Making Of The Man Who Rebuilds Faces
Copyright © 2016 by Kofi Boahene, MD

info.drboahene@gmail.com

ISBN: 978-0-9974930-0-9

Copies are available at special discounts for bulk purchases in the
United States by corporations, institutions, and other organizations.
For more information, please contact the publisher.

Editorial, production, and publishing services provided by
Platform Press
Winans Kuenstler Publishing, LLC
93 East Court Street
Doylestown, Pennsylvania 18901
(215) 500-1989
www.WKPublishing.com

Printed in the United States

All the rivers run into the sea; yet the sea is not full;
unto the place from whence the rivers come,
thither they return again.

—Ecclesiastes 1:7 KJV

TABLE OF CONTENTS

AUTHOR'S NOTE

On November 1, 2015, three years after starting the process of writing this book, I completed the final editorial work and forwarded the finished manuscript to my publisher. For what seemed like endless days, I had been up late recalling, writing, and correcting.

Once the task was complete I felt a bit of emptiness and doubt. I questioned my motivation and wondered whether readers would be all that interested in yet another memoir.

Then, as I often do at the end of each day, I checked my email and found this message from an unfamiliar sender.

Hello Dr. Boahene,

I am a student from Nepal, a graduate from China. I found your story when I was all burnt out of studying and needed some inspiration and what a joy I felt after watching your video ...

I have received hundreds of such emails over the past seven years since "The Long Way Here," the story of my journey to medicine, was first filmed as a short video and published as a profile in the *Johns Hopkins Magazine* by Ramsey Flynn, a National Magazine Award winner and author of the book *Cry From the Deep*, an investigative look into Russia's Kursk submarine disaster in 2008. Flynn wrote about my odyssey as a young African student from Ghana, through my experiences studying in Russia to one of the great houses of medicine—Hopkins—in the United States.

The article and video generated several requests for me to write the full version of my story. A few years later, photojournalist Jessica Ellis produced a half-hour special on my work as a medical missionary for a CNN International segment on its program *African Voices*. It was titled "The Man Who Rebuilds Faces."

Since it aired I have received hundreds of messages from students around the world seeking advice, and some from parents looking for ways to encourage their children's educational goals. I answer the majority of those emails and now, in this book, I have provided a more complete response.

Of the many people who believed I had a worthwhile story to share, Dr. Elfreda Massie, a former superintendent of the Washington, DC schools, is the one who finally nudged me into action. Elfreda was visiting the Hopkins campus and passed by my office to ask how my book was coming along. At the time I had organized my thoughts and compiled a few notes about how the book might flow, but had yet to take the first step.

I gave Elfreda the same excuse I offered a year earlier: "I have been too busy with work." This time she urged me to roll with the momentum. She introduced me to Foster Winans, a veteran book editor, who helped me bring my story to life. I am grateful for Foster and his team at Winans Kuenstler Publishing for all the effort they put into this project. My sincere gratitude goes to Raquel Pidal for helping coordinate interviews across continents and diligently editing the final product.

I have retraced the past forty or so years of my life and what made it into these pages is a collection of stories and events that shaped my worldview, guided me on my path, and inspired me toward realizing my improbable dreams. In recording these tales I am continuing a family tradition of storytelling, passing history from one generation to the next, a practice that before now was done orally.

My children enjoyed hearing me tell them folktales common to West African and Caribbean cultures when they were little. Now, as they approach their teenaged years, I've begun to tell them about my days in boarding school in Ghana and my adventures in the former Soviet Union. With the book nearing completion, when they asked for another story I've been telling them to wait for the book. They have grown impatient. "Dad," my son James asked me one day, "just how long does it take to write a book, anyway?"

Jonathan, the younger twin by a few minutes, has been saying for the past three years that he wants to attend Oxford University and become an English professor and author. I hope that one day he will add to this story his own experiences as he strives to fulfill his dreams.

Thus, it is to my children—Akua, James, Jonathan, and Nana—that this work is dedicated.

A story is written in the sands of time long before it is rendered in ink on paper. Mine spans three continents and includes appearances by numerous Samaritans around the world who played a helping role. I could fill a book just thanking all those who deserve acknowledgment. I have chosen instead to name just a few, hoping that all the others will know in their hearts that as I write this I am thinking about them with gratitude.

The family of the late Dr. Edusa, an ear, nose, and throat (ENT) doctor in Ghana, encouraged me to take up the opportunity to study in Russia in spite of the fact that it wasn't part of my grand plan. I last saw Dr. Edusa in London in 1992 when I left Moscow amid political unrest there, uncertain what my next steps should be. His advice and wisdom helped me navigate some tough days.

The new families who adopted me when I moved to the US include the Lennons and the Amoakohenes. They showered me with love, support, and their prayers.

Esi Asante, a woman whose heart overflows with selfless kindness, kept me fed and provided me with a safe place to live during the crucial first months of medical school.

Many friends generously agreed to be interviewed for the book, enhancing my memory and adding important details. Some of the stories I've chosen reflect my appreciation for colleagues and support staff at Johns Hopkins Hospital who collaborate with me every day in caring for the sick and discovering innovative ways of solving difficult surgical problems.

Humanitarian medical missions have taken me places I would have never dreamed of being able to visit. These mission groups—Children's Surgery International, Foundation for Special Surgery, Face the Future Foundation, and Grace Missions—have allowed me to experience and share the privilege of caring for the underserved in some of the most remote places on the planet.

To honor those who taught me so muchand challenged me to think innovatively, I have tried to pass on what I learned to others. My students, residents, and fellows have embraced the idea that questioning convention makes them more effective. They have become sources of continuing inspiration for me and others.

I feel particular gratitude for the family of my late chemistry teacher, Jerry Manion, for all he did to make my first steps in medicine possible.

My trusting patients and families remind me daily of the

bravery of the human spirit and the miracle of healing. Their courage is a source of strength and keeps me motivated to continuously research new, more effective solutions for their complex problems.

Lastly, I am thankful to my family—parents, siblings, and my wife, Adjoa—who have been honest critics, enthusiastic cheerleaders, careful fact-checkers, and helpful memory joggers, and who have allowed me to share their stories with mine.

THE ICONS AT THE BEGINNING OF EACH CHAPTER are **Adinkra** symbols, traditional drawings originally created by the Akan (Ashanti or Asante) people of Ghana and the Gyaman of Cote d'Ivoire in West Africa. Each icon is a representation of a distinct philosophy, proverb, belief, or aspect of history. Adinkra symbols are used to communicate evocative messages that represent wisdom, norms, culture, and life in society. A key to the meaning of each of the Adinkra symbols can be found at the end of this book and at http://adinkraproject.com.

Source: The Noun Project, NCOC Ghana, Wikipedia

INTRODUCTION

However far the stream flows, it never forgets its source.

That proverb is familiar among the peoples of West Africa, the region from which nine million or so souls were uprooted and exiled during the Atlantic slave trade. A great many of them had their last glimpse of Africa when they passed through the infamous "Door Of No Return" at Elmina Castle, which sits on the coast of the ancestral homeland of my ethnic group, the Akan, and within the Akan, my tribe—the Ashanti of Ghana.

The proverb captures the dichotomy between the bitter and the sweet in our history. It evokes the grief of separation experienced by so many displaced Africans over the centuries. It also reminds us that family, faith, heritage, and tradition—their sources—inspired them to create new, productive lives and communities in foreign and often hostile lands.

Lucky as I was to be born into a more civilized world, the proverb nevertheless speaks to me and to the million of others who, like myself, are citizens of the African diaspora. Many of us left as teenagers and young adults to pursue professional goals abroad. We took with us a strong devotion to familial and cultural traditions that define us wherever we settle.

Overseas, Africans show their devotion by lending their skills and sharing their good fortunes helping their families back home and creating opportunities for future generations. Many, as I did, will only marry a native African. The concept that it takes a village to raise a child, another African proverb, seems to be baked into the DNA of many African societies.

This natural instinct among the Ashanti, to stay connected to our heritage, is not unique but it is unusually fervent compared with most fragmented ethnic groups. A 2005 study commissioned through the United States Agency for International Development found that the typical emigrant sends money back home at a decreasing rate the longer he or she has lived abroad. The longer that overseas Ghanaians have been away, the more money they send back, and the more frequently they send it. About half of us invest in Ghana and maintain real estate there. The study also found that a majority of Ghanaians living in the United States and Great Britain visit Ghana at least once a year.

Like so many emigrants who have made the journey to America from some far corner of the world, mine has been improbable in retrospect and at times dramatic. I come from an established family with deep roots that, during the first few years of my life, had an ascending narrative and would have been considered upper middle class in the context of the times and place. Only one or two generations removed from small-village life in Ghana's tropical highlands, my parents and their peers were aspiring professionals and entrepreneurs. My father was always an avid reader and worked as a book salesman before becoming involved with a successful pharmaceutical business during my elementary school years.

Ours is a tribal society with British-style institutions left over from the colonial period, which was officially extinguished with independence in 1957. The Ashanti narrative goes back about a thousand years, has colorful traditions and mythology, was once the wealthiest in Africa due to its gold mines, and traditionally was a matriarchal society.

When I was about ten there was a military coup and our fortunes reversed. As a result, we were quite poor during the second half of my youth. Nevertheless, when our parents weren't praying for my siblings and I to have a better life—which my mother did every morning when she first got up—they were always encouraging us to set our sights high.

It has been a long road from being the child who wakes to his mother's prayers each morning to where I am now, performing complex surgeries and medical missionary work. There were twists, turns, lucky breaks, and near misses, any one of which could have dashed my dreams. I like to think that it was my mother's prayers that made the difference. Her faith gave me the determination to keep trying when life got complicated, which it often did. As a result, my career path has been circuitous.

For more than half my life I have lived and worked a hemisphere away from home. There have been long periods, up to nine years, when financial and other complications made it impossible to visit. I have often felt the ache of separation.

What kept me going were the echoes of my mother's prayers, a determination to live up to my parents' expectations, and an obligation to fulfill the aspirations of my faith by using my skills in service to others. Since completing my medical training and joining the faculty at Johns Hopkins University Hospital in Baltimore, Maryland, I have participated in numerous medical missions to Ghana, among other African countries, as well as Peru, Bangladesh, and Mexico.

The nature of my specialty, facial reconstructive surgery, and the fact that children comprise a large segment of my patients, have together given me the opportunity and privilege to be the instrument of dramatic change in many families. For example, one of the simplest surgeries in my toolkit—fixing cleft upper lips in infants—can take as little as forty-five minutes in the operating room yet completely alter the course and quality of a life.

In recent years several missionary groups have run large-scale and, at times, distressingly graphic advertising campaigns to raise funds for treating children born with this deformity. Everyone, it seems, has seen them. The reason for the focus on this particular deformity is that without the simple operation an otherwise perfectly healthy child is at high risk of dying. It is difficult and sometimes impossible for these babies to nurse and many succumb to malnutrition and disease.

In some societies, a child born with a cleft lip is a source of shame and embarrassment, so these children are kept hidden, never allowed outside, and sometimes starved to death. A girl born with a cleft lip will never marry. In superstitious cultures the mother is said to be cursed. Children who manage to survive infancy with unrepaired lips are always ostracized and suffer severe psychological problems.

That is just one sub-category of surgery that my colleagues

and I perform during our missions. In my field, some patients come to us with ghastly facial wounds that won't heal, defects after cancer surgery, or any number of congenital abnormalities and disfiguring growths that, in addition to their suffering, make them pariahs in their communities.

Success for me is defined as the moment a patient who has never shown her face in public feels comfortable doing so, or when a child with nerve damage is able for the first time to smile back at his parents. It is the most rewarding work I can imagine, as close as one can get to living a childhood dream.

My interest in medicine officially began when I was about ten years old, although I had already developed a feel for the language and protocols of healing from watching my father. He was a chemist, the British term for a type of pharmacist, who—in at a time and place when regulation of pharmaceuticals was practically nonexistent—filled prescriptions and sold medications out of our house. You could say I grew up in a drugstore.

Although he wasn't a doctor and you wouldn't have called his customers patients, people often trusted him to diagnose and to recommend medications. Sometimes I even filled in for him when he was busy with his church missionary work and a customer showed up with symptoms of malaria.

One of the memorable events in my childhood was the day my father brought home a set of encyclopedias. An avid reader, I spent hours with my nose buried in those heavy, thick volumes with their musty leather covers.

During one of my browsing sessions my eye snagged on an entry about a famous hospital in America. The Mayo Clinic had been started in 1889 in Minnesota by a British-American physician, Dr. William W. Mayo. Dr. Mayo had been a chemist before becoming a doctor. His two sons grew up to become surgeons and they joined Dr. Mayo, thus inventing the modern group practice and sowing the seeds of one of the world's most recognized and respected medical institutions.

Reading about the Mayo Clinic struck a chord in me. The next time I saw my chums I announced that I was going to work at that hospital when I grew up. Perhaps it was the connection I made with having a chemist in the family, and the idea that I might follow in his footsteps, helping others. Perhaps I imagined my siblings doing the same and we would all work together in our own clinic.

I had no concept of the geographical and bureaucratic chasm that separated me from the Mayo Clinic, nor did I grasp the infinitesimal odds that somehow I, a little African boy from an impoverished former British colony, could end up there. In time, I forgot about Mayo. The memory only came back some fifteen years later when, by chance, I was offered the opportunity to intern there.

You could say I have realized my dream but I am still young and the dream has been embellished. My goal is to raise the funds necessary to build a modern surgical teaching hospital in Ghana to address the most critical issue facing much of Africa—access for ordinary people to good surgical care. I hope to facilitate the training of Ghanaian and other African doctors who will find the challenges and opportunities they seek at home instead of having to go abroad, as I did, and then come back as missionaries.

In memorializing my journey I hope to inspire my four young children, who have had the advantages that go along with being born in America but whose parents were both born in Ghana. However far their streams may flow, I hope they will recognize, even if they can't remember, the source.

—Dr. Derek Kofi Owusu Boahene
Baltimore, Maryland 2016

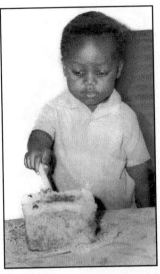

My first surgery, performed at the age of two, on a birthday cake. A big success, although afterward the patient was nowhere to be found.

A growing family: Back row, from left—George, Elaine, and me (smiling). Front row, from left—Francis and Akwasi.

My mother, Helena.

My father, James, with me (right)
and my sister Elaine.

My parents with the youngest of my siblings, Kofi Owusu (left) and Yvette.

CHAPTER 1:
WHAT'S ONE LIFE,
MORE OR LESS?

Our friend was bleeding to death and no one at the hospital seemed to care.

My schoolmates and I kept steady pressure on his wounds. In spite of a phobia I'd had since childhood about the sight of blood, that was the moment that set me on the path to becoming a doctor. My father had planted the idea when I was five. My mother nurtured it and it had grown into a dream. Now that I had my hands bloodied trying to save a life, I had no trouble imagining being one.

We were a group of four or five classmates—about sixteen years old—at an all-boys' British-style boarding school in Kumasi, the largest city in Ghana and the historical capital of the Ashanti people, my tribal ethnic group. One day in 1987, during my final year, a classmate got hold of a motorbike and, in violation of school policy, darted off on a helmet-less joy ride around the campus. He was having a grand time, laughing and showing off his skills, when he lost control and took a very bad spill, landing head first. He was alive but bleeding from multiple wounds.

A group of us picked him up as gently as we could and carried him—limp, moaning, his shirt front blood-soaked—through streets full of gawkers to the nearest hospital. We burst through the emergency room doors like soldiers rushing a wounded comrade to a waiting helicopter. A sea of weary faces of the sick and injured turned to see what the fuss was about.

There was no sign of a doctor. We tried to buttonhole a nurse to politely let her know our friend needed to be seen right away. She was distracted and waved us off. I had never been exposed to the healthcare system in Ghana and this apparent disinterest upset me.

The staff seemed oblivious to the urgency of the situation. No matter how much we pleaded, the nurses just shrugged. "There's nothing we can do. You'll just have to wait." To our naive and terrified ears they were saying, *If he dies, what's one life more or less?* Today I understand how that can happen in a crowded, understaffed hospital in a struggling nation like Ghana. At the time it shocked my sensibilities that anyone could possibly think that way.

A brain drain, typical throughout Africa, left Ghana perennially short of physicians. Those who had been able to complete their medical training in Ghana tended to emigrate as soon as they were able. The country was under military rule, the government had changed eight times in fifteen years, and the politics were such that doctors were under-paid and overworked. Given the opportunity of a better life abroad, many have taken it.

We boys were lucky that the father of one of our group was a surgeon who ran a small private hospital. This boy was used to seeing his dad do surgeries so he knew the basics and showed us what to do.

We sat there with our moaning friend, our hands and clothes smeared with his blood, holding hastily repurposed shirts and other clothing scraps to his wounds, all of us anxious and scared. He had a number of fractured bones in his face and deep cuts over eyes, brow, and on his forehead. We were all numb with shock.

After what seemed an indecent amount of time, our friend finally got the treatment he needed, was admitted to the hospital, and our rescue mission was complete. With my mates, I walked the six miles back to school clutching one of the sticky T-shirts we had used as a makeshift tamponade—a surgical plug—to stanch his bleeding. When we approached the campus and passed through a nearby orchard, I finally tossed it into the bushes.

The act of discarding the bloody shirt became symbolic, a turning point in my life. Looking back on the experience years later with the benefit of my medical training, I realize I had inadvertently, or maybe intuitively, employed a method of behavioral therapy to deal with my hemophobia—the fear of blood.

A phobia is the irrational and intense fear of a specific object or situation. Common phobias include heights, the dark, germs, spiders, and the sight of blood. Phobias are quite different from the self-preservation instinct one feels when faced with actual danger, like a hungry crocodile or a loaded gun.

One of the treatments for phobia used by behavioral therapists is to expose patients to the thing that triggers it, in a safe and controlled environment. "Flooding therapy" is the immersion of the patient in the fear reflex until he or she becomes inured to it and the emotional response fades. In my desperation to help our friend, I was literally immersed—flooded—in so much blood that my phobia had been cured.

That was a monumental revelation—I could deal with the sight of blood after all. In fact, I could deal with it so well that I resolved to become a doctor so that I could help keep that situation—needing urgent care that wasn't available—from happening to someone else.

Our injured friend survived but was in the hospital for such a protracted time that he missed almost the entire last year of school, a terrible setback for such an ambitious student. It was compounded by the fact that he had been considered quite handsome, so much so that we had nicknamed him Michael Jackson. His healed wounds left his face badly scarred, a trauma that would stay with him the rest of his life.

It was just a coincidence, but one I took particular note of, that years later I would become a doctor specializing in fixing such facial disfigurements. Knowing what I do today, there is so much that could have been done to restore his appearance and self-confidence. It was also pure coincidence that when I began returning to Ghana on surgical missions, I ended up performing some facial reconstructive surgeries in that very same hospital. Today it is well-equipped but still struggles to retain a full complement of skilled staff.

Across the board in Africa that is the single biggest problem with health care—there aren't enough medical professionals to serve all the people who need it. In Ghana, for example, there are fewer than a hundred spots open each year for those who want to study medicine without having to leave home. In a nation of 26 million, that's a per-capita ratio of about one new doctor each year for 250,000 people.

The per-capita ratio of first year medical students in the US is about sixteen for 250,000, and that's spoken of as a shortage in a nation with the most modern infrastructure and procedures. This enormous gap in Africa is on top of chronic problems such as the AIDS virus, the spread of infectious tropical diseases like Ebola, and the general scarcity of potable water and proper sanitation.

The world has focused its attention on infectious diseases in Africa, but the scarcity of specialist surgeons is an equally urgent problem. An African who suffers a serious leg injury may well end up with amputation as the first response because there aren't the microsurgeons available who know how to repair blood vessels and nerves to save a limb.

My baptism in my schoolmate's misfortune left a deep impression and dovetailed with the experiences I'd had growing up, watching and helping my father in his role as a chemist. The regulatory scheme was quite lax, reflecting in part the traditional African homespun, herbal approach to treating illness. Things are changing, but even today a Ghanaian chemist often plays the role of diagnostician.

My father's regular customers would come to him for advice first because it was so hard to see a doctor. Certain ailments, like loose stools, were common in a region fertile for food-borne diseases like cholera. By the age of ten or eleven I knew what medication you needed if you had that problem.

Sometimes a person would come to our house complaining of headaches and fever, symptoms associated with malaria, another common illness. I grew up knowing the medications for treating malaria from hearing the same story over and over again. I paid close enough attention to my father's work that if he was unavailable when someone came in asking for a malaria medicine that was out of stock, I knew the alternative drug that would do the same thing.

In addition to my interest in my father's work and the jolt of reality I got when my friend had his accident, there was a third and most important influence in shaping my career choice. It was my desire to become the man my father was, to manifest the intent expressed in another Ashanti proverb: When you follow in the path of your father, you learn to walk like him.

Our culture seems to be quite fond of the paths and streams that link us to our heritage. The emphasis we put on those connections reflects tribal pride mixed with a cultural tendency toward humility. Only recently liberated from nearly five hundred years of the slave trade and colonialism, virtually all West Africans can trace their roots to a remote jungle village—the humble source of their stream, the beginning of their father's and mother's paths.

This devotion to family and elders reflects an obligation we're born with, to honor and emulate our role models, to know and add to our family narratives, and to live our ideals and faith. My parents, perhaps a bit more than other families, were quite deliberate in raising their eight children. They were consistent and confident role models, their ideals were constant and they practiced them every day for us to see. My father was a pastor and we were all active church members. We also had an inner church at home. As a family we would gather at the kitchen table in the evenings and read the Bible together, discussing and debating the meaning and message of each passage.

My prejudice is obvious, but I doubt any child they raised could have become anything less than a competent, loving, successful adult. All eight of their children are proof of concept. Six of us are in healthcare—two surgeons, an anesthesiologist, a pharmacy administrator, a nurse, and a medical technologist. One brother is a software engineer and another is a businessman in Ghana. All of us faced significant hurdles along the way.

As the firstborn of eight, responsibility came early to me. From the time I was old enough to hold my first sibling in my arms, a sister, I became the third parent of an ever-growing family.

Until I was ten, my father's chemist business was profitable. We lived in the city and, by local standards at the time, were uppermiddle class. My father, the youngest of six kids growing up in a subsistence farming village, had come a long way to get where he was. Although his father died when he was three years old, he grew up among many loving adults—his mother, four older sisters and an older brother, plus extended family members and neighbors.

He came from a village in the Ashanti Kingdom (sometimes referred to as the Ashanti Empire) which at the time was still part of the British-ruled Gold Coast colony that became Ghana upon independence in 1957.

As colonists, the British were relatively benevolent. They were the first of the great powers to abolish slavery in the early 1800s, when West Africa was a principal export point for slaves being sent to the Americas. The British brought with them a passion for education so that by the 1940s the colony had one of the best and most accessible educational systems in Africa. New schools were popping up in the district where my father lived and he was able to enroll in one.

Getting an education was a big deal. Everyone expected my father to get the best marks and he did, while also keeping up with his farm chores, working in the fields and carrying the harvest to town on market days.

When he graduated from high school he moved to the capital, Accra, to begin his career and start a family. When I was growing up he often referred to his early experiences and to his mother. Other people we knew who had come from the countryside would sometimes tease me, telling me how helpless a city kid like myself would be if I had to live back in the village.

When I was eight years old, I got a chance to disprove this assumption when it was decided that one of my brothers and I would spend a summer in my father's home village, Nsuta, living with our grandmother. We kids carefully packed our clothes, soccer jersey, and football, got into my father's Peugeot, and a hired man drove us the eight-hour expedition from Accra.

The mostly dirt road seemed to go on forever, hours and hours of passing farms, women walking along the road in brightly colored outfits with parcels balanced on their heads, through rain forests with soaring, majestic trees, and

many villages that looked like the ones I'd seen in maga-
zines—mud huts, thatched roofs, muddy lanes, and chickens
squawking as we drove by. Was Nsuta that kind of village? I
began to have second thoughts.

Our first major stop was Kumasi, the second largest city
in Ghana and the capital of the Ashanti region. By the time
we got there I was feeling anxious enough that I wanted to
speak with my parents. The driver placed the call for me from
a phone booth and handed me the receiver. I began peppering
my dad with questions about what was going to happen, and
what it would be like. He seemed distressingly unconcerned.

"Dad, when we get to the village, are we going to stay in
a clay house or a cement house?"

Raucous laughter erupted in the background—my
mother's voice.

"It'll be a clay house, of course," my father said.

"Nice and cool during the day and warm at night," my
mother called out, chuckling.

They didn't seem to grasp the potential peril.

"But Dad, what if someone breaks through the clay wall
and steals my stuff or takes me?"

As only an eight-year-old can be, I was truly scared and
feeling vulnerable. My father said all the right things.

"Remember, I grew up in that very same house where
you're going to stay with your grandmother. I slept there
thousands of nights and no one kidnapped me, or took my
things. You should see where your father comes from. You
should see where your grandmother sleeps."

I saw where my grandmother slept that summer, and I
earned my stripes as a village boy. I learned to till soil, plant

yams, harvest cassavas, weave baskets from palm fronds, and barter trade. That last skill came in handy when I got back home and started to do the daily marketing for my mother. I had become a crafty negotiator.

My father reminded me from time to time about the day he left Nsuta to begin his working life far away. He was about nineteen years old, going to work as a bookseller for a department store in Accra. He loved reading, so it was a good fit.

It was understood in the village that he was unlikely to ever again live there permanently. The day he left, his mother summoned him to her bedroom and pointed to the straw mat on the floor. It was where she'd slept nearly every night of her adult life, where she lay when she was sick, where she had given birth to my father.

"My son, no matter where you go or what you do, never forget where your mother sleeps."

More profound than any proverb or saying, that moment became a defining principle for him—never forget your roots, never surrender to hubris. He told this story more than once and the reverent way he told it made it profound in my life as well. My hope is that, in one fashion or another, it will become profound in the lives of my children as well.

My father's storytelling skill comes in part from his charismatic demeanor. It made him such a good salesman that a pair of book-browsing Brits recruited him from the store where he worked to be their senior sales executive for an expanding chain of chemists—drug stores. After several successful years, and marrying my mother, he opened his own shop.

My mother was also the youngest of a large family—seven children—and a twin. She, however, was born in the big city, Kumasi, and her father was a government bureaucrat. The family moved wherever he was needed so she had seen quite a bit of the country. Her father also died young, after which she lived with her oldest brother, who worked in the diplomatic corps. There was no money for secondary school so she went to work as a teller in a central bank.

My father was twenty-seven years old at the time but considered himself unready financially and otherwise for marriage. One day a friend insisted that my dad meet that fellow's sister, who was twenty-one. My mother and father hit it off and in spite of her family's disapproval—they were a few rungs higher on the social ladder—they got married. It proved to be a good match. I inherited my father's shyness and circumspection and my mother's nurturing instincts and strong will.

My parents were a true team. They often started their day praying together in their room, followed by family devotion, a core ritual. "A family without devotion is like a house without a roof," my mother would say. The alarm was always set to six o'clock . Before breakfast and our other morning routines, we all gathered in our living room, sang some inspiring hymns or spirituals, read a Bible passage, prayed for each other and for others, and asked for God's guidance for the day.

My father has always been active in the church, first as a deacon and later as a pastor and an enthusiastic missionary among his own people. In his forties, he attended seminary school, taking classes at night and on weekends. The members of the church he pastors came to calling him Evangelist James.

He is a liaison and coordinator with international

missionary groups that send him volunteers. He puts them to work building churches in the smallest villages and putting to good use their civic and community development skills, whether it be digging a drainage ditch, helping on farms, or teaching algebra. Hundreds of people from all points of the compass have eaten at my parents' dining table, especially from the US, which, after the UK, is home to the largest contingent of the Ghanaian diaspora.

In addition to building churches, my father builds missionaries, of which I am one. Young people from abroad spend up to six months living with my parents, working hard, getting to know the culture, and learning the finer points of being a good missionary. I sometimes think of my father as a missionary doctor—he has a clinical eye, a believer's passion, and a Samaritan heart. I have been following in his path my whole life and striving to walk like him.

Soon after the experience with my friend at the hospital I began plotting my next step. Through my father's missionary network, we had developed long-distance friendships with church members in the United States.

Some of my classmates who had relatives living in the UK and the US were applying to schools abroad and it was well-known that the odds of getting into an America college were slim. Even were I to be so lucky, there would be many complications. Nevertheless, I regularly visited the American Education Center in Accra for about a year, picking up the latest university catalogs. When I had exhausted the reading material there, I did the same at the British consulate.

Whenever I had some spare cash I would fill out an application, get an international money order for the fee, and send it off. When I didn't have the money, I'd fill out the application anyway and send it off with a note asking if they could waive the fee. I didn't know how I would do it, but I was determined to get to medical school.

CHAPTER 2:
THE PROMISE

Growing up in an emerging, post-colonial African nation has had its advantages. Many of the habits and skills that became instinctive in my youth out of necessity have served me well in my career as a physician, surgeon, and medical missionary.

Patience was essential. Without it life would have been intolerable. Money and opportunity was limited by a mostly subsistence economy and an unsettled political scheme punctuated by coups. One of the positive legacies of British rule was a good educational system. It was and remains a common aspiration of parents that their kids get a university degree and join the professional class. People like my father, who grew up in a rural village, worked hard and saved everything they could to be able to pay tuitions for me and my seven siblings.

Patience took the form of knowing that even if I was

hungry after school I had to wait until my mother had cooked dinner and it was time for everyone to sit down. Walking home from classes you could hear the pounding of cassava for fufu, the basic starch of the Ghanaian diet, from kitchens throughout the neighborhood.

After school and after we had done our homework, the neighborhood kids would gather for a game of soccer. Many of us gave our parents fits by turning our newly purchased T-shirts into team jerseys by writing our numbers on the back with markers.

Snacks and sodas that are everywhere today were relative luxuries. When we were thirsty, we drank water. A snack might be had by climbing one of the huge mango trees in our neighborhood—something I was adept at—to see if any ripe ones had escaped the attention of the bugs and birds. Sometimes we'd work together to shake a palm tree and dislodge a few coconuts.

In the yard of the house next to ours where Joe, a childhood friend, lived there stood a prodigious mango tree, so tall that my parents had forbidden me to climb it. One day after school a group of us hungry kids decided the yellow mangoes in that tree were just begging us to harvest a few.

We took turns shaking branches and throwing stones to try to knock them down but something more was required. With one of us assigned to be the lookout for approaching parents, I was boosted up so I could reach the first branch. From there I climbed all the way up to the top where the ripest mangoes would be found.

I was busy plucking and dropping fruit to my coconspirators below when a voice shouted, "Kofi! Your mum is coming!"

In my rush to avoid punishment I stepped onto a branch that turned out to be dead. It snapped and I tumbled to the ground, landing with a thump that knocked the breath out of me. When I came to, my mum was standing over me, her faced creased with worry.

That evening, satisfied that there had been no lasting injury, my parents got out our Bible and made me recite Proverbs 22:15: "Foolishness is bound in the heart of a child; but the rod of correction shall drive it far from him."

Until I was about ten, our family lived in a comfortable, walled compound that had six bedrooms, a family room, a living room, and verandas where you could sit on a stifling day out of the sun or stay dry during the wet season. Attached to the main house was a bungalow that the British called the "boys' quarters," where servants would have lived. In our family it was often occupied by grandparents, aunts and uncles, nieces and nephews, cousins, and the occasional family friend or stranger in need of shelter and food.

During this period, when my father's chemist business flourished, our family helped just about anyone who asked, and without ceremony. People just dropped by, often timing their visits with the evening meal.

A knock at the door might be a man from the rural village where my father and his family came from, asking us to host his daughter and help her learn a trade, an opportunity that could only be found in a major city like Accra. These young women were entrusted to us because their families knew we would keep them safe and well cared for. Such tribal and village extended-family networks are common in Ghana.

There would always be some activity at home: people

coming and going, food being prepared, relatives and others pitching in with chores or taking care of kids. It was a culturally rich environment, very much the village that the old proverb says it takes to raise a child. At any given time there might be a dozen people in our house.

My parents also occasionally took in strangers who were in desperate straits. Beginning in the 1970s, the country of Chad experienced a devastating and extended drought that drove thousands of starving people across Chad's borders. A number found their way to Accra, walking the entire 1,500 or so miles to get there. A few ended up in our home.

It was my father's good fortune to be able to provide food and shelter to those down on their luck, and opportunity to aspiring young people on their way up in the world. Most of the young women from the villages wanted to learn dressmaking so they could find work as seamstresses. My parents bought some sewing machines and recruited an expert to teach the women how to operate them.

My father's success in business—in addition to the chemist shop we had a large poultry farm—made it possible for us kids to go to private schools that were academically more rigorous and would give us opportunities we might not have had otherwise. He even paid the tuition of other students who were less fortunate but showed promise.

His generosity worried family friends who often advised my parents, "You guys would be better off if you sent your kids to public school and did not spend all that money." They wouldn't hear of it.

My father told me more than once, "When I die, I may have nothing to pass on to you as an inheritance. I'm not so wealthy that I'm going to leave you houses and land. But if I give you a good education, nobody can take that away."

Everything changed beginning in 1979 when a military coup disrupted the economy and changed the political landscape. In the days following the coup, foreigners fled Ghana, taking their capital with them. Among them were my father's British employers who hastily handed the pharmacy company over to the local employees. Soon after that my father quit to concentrate on running his chemist shop, which was attached to the rented house we lived in. My parents had signed and paid for a long-term lease with the owner, a woman in her sixties.

By a stroke of terrible luck, the landlady died rather suddenly. One day her two daughters showed up declaring in loud, unpleasant voices that we would have to leave. They wanted the house back.

My father decided it was time we had our own house so he bought a plot of land in an affluent part of town. The construction plans were drawn and the builders showed up to begin work only to find a group of hired thugs with machetes and soldiers with guns. They were there to enforce a claim by someone else who had been sold the same plot. My parents had been duped in a common fraud. We lost the land and the money.

Against the backdrop of the gathering civil chaos, a gang of thieves invaded our house one night and held us at gunpoint, huddled in a corner, while they stole my father's inventory of medications, money, personal effects, and furniture. We lost everything of value.

With no other resources, my parents did what they had

to—my dad started driving his private car as a taxi and later bought a van, hiring himself out to transport goods from the airport. My mother went back to work as a teller in a bank. We were being evicted with nowhere to go. All the people my parents had helped over the years vanished and we were on our own with what little help we could get from close friends and family.

We moved into a small two-room house—my parents, five kids (three would be born later), and what remained of our possessions. The chemist shop gone, my father sold what medications he could from a corner of one of the rooms. On weekends I packed a few staples into a cart—cough medicine, paracetamol (for fever and pain), and milk of magnesia—and trundled from house to house peddling.

About six months after we moved, we were robbed again. My father's friends began to refer to him as Job. He remained patient and continued to trust God in spite of his trials and tribulations. From then on I prayed each night with my heart aching, "God, give us a home of our own. If you get us out of this, I promise I will devote my life to serving you."

My parents were perfect role models for how to meet adversity with persistence and dignity. I never heard either of them complain. I recall a happy childhood in a loving family but our travails helped me mature early, along with being the firstborn. Before I was even ten years old my dad had entrusted me with the combination to his safe, telling me, "You are my firstborn. If anything happens, this is where things are."

My parents slowly worked their way back to some financial stability and after two years we moved to a three-bedroom house in a better part of the city.

Store-bought toys were mostly unheard of among my friends and schoolmates, so we invented our entertainment. After a passing shower we would race sticks in the gutters. We'd scout the neighborhood for discarded tins, pieces of rope, sections of pipe, a bent bicycle wheel, a plastic bucket lid—whatever looked like it had potential or might complete some gizmo we had dreamed up.

The most popular toy for an African boy to make was a car. These were often fashioned out of bits of packing-case wire to make the outline of a car about a foot long, complete with steering mechanism that you could control with a wire steering wheel while standing. With jar or tin can lids and bottoms repurposed into wheels, boys would race each other in the street.

My cars were more ambitious. I cut apart empty powdered-chocolate cans and cut, bent, and crimped them into panels. To rivet the panels together I took the pieces of tin I wanted to join, put one atop the other, and then hammered a nail through both. Remove the nail, crimp the edges of the hole, and that was a reliable rivet.

The windscreen was fashioned out of the clear plastic collar stays that come in new shirts. Clear plastic bottles provided lens material for headlights, red plastic for tail lights. I even rigged up working lights inside with a battery and some bulbs rescued from an old radio.

Those experiences shaped how I approach complex, difficult cases that defy conventional treatment, a common occurrence in my specialty—otolaryngology. I diagnose and treat conditions and diseases that occur from the shoulders up—neck, throat, mouth, sinuses, ears, face: everything but the brain. What distinguishes otolaryngology from most other specialties is that it requires medical as well as surgical skills, and the part of the body we treat is the intersection of all our vital functions and systems.

My subspecialty is facial reconstructive surgery, one of the most demanding and, for me, rewarding. Whether fixing a simple lip defect or removing an embedded growth—anything involving the face—the goal is to make precise incisions where they will be the least noticeable. Then we meticulously suture the wounds so that when they are healed they will be as undetectable as possible. All this must be done without damaging the many nerves and other structures that control the shape and movement of the face.

Unlike most other types of surgery, facial reconstruction has a psychological factor that for some procedures requires a pre-operation mental health evaluation to make sure the patient is prepared for change. Our emotional lives are so often shaped by what we see in the mirror or what is reflected in the eyes of others. Fixing a complex deformity or a disfiguring condition like facial nerve damage is nearly always a positive life-changing experience. But occasionally a patient becomes traumatized when they look in the mirror and no longer recognize themselves.

The complexity of these surgeries intrigues me. I like the challenge of trying to solve the unsolvable and by doing so enriching a life. Once in a while that leads to an exciting discovery. A couple of years ago a neurosurgeon colleague came to me about a patient who had a benign but growing tumor at the bottom of the brain. The standard procedure to reach and remove it would have been to cut open the skull, an operation that is hard on the patient, involves a long period of recovery, and can cause irreversible side effects.

The site of this tumor was behind one of the patient's eyes. Sitting at my desk later, I picked up the model skull that is always at my elbow, squinted and sighted through one of the eye sockets. I realized that by gently nudging the eyeball aside, it might be possible to reach the tumor through the socket. Then, using the latest miniaturized surgical tools, we could remove it without disassembling the face or leaving visible scars. The operation was a success and became the subject of a published paper, opening up possible solutions for similar procedures that might otherwise require "cracking the skull."

When I'm thinking about a case like that I'm reminded of the boy I was, roaming the streets of Accra, Ghana, making things out of found junk. I'm hardly unique in this. Many successful surgeons who came from similar backgrounds talk about making their own toys and growing up learning to make do with what you've got. My children have every possible advantage, and I can't help wishing I could somehow give them that experience.

My younger brother, James, who also became a facial plastic and reconstructive surgeon, was a master as a child at fixing the unfixable. When a light bulb had burned out and was about to be discarded, he would fiddle with it until he somehow got it working again. Today, like myself, he rebuilds faces.

Ghanaian parents who aspire for their children to become professionals are partial to medicine or law since those are the most respected and accessible. My parents began to lobby me when I was about five or six, but I resisted the idea for a long time because I found the sight of blood so unnerving.

A voracious reader, I often spent hours leafing through a set of encyclopedias that my father had bought me for a birthday. In spite of my fear of blood, when I read the entry for The Mayo Clinic I was so inspired that the next day I told my friends I would work there when I was grown up. I hoped there was a kind of doctor that didn't have to deal with blood so I could please my parents while avoiding my phobia.

As oldest child, I learned early on to be responsible for others and to think for myself. After we moved into the smaller house my mother had her hands full. In addition to helping her with the little ones, she would send me to the open-air market to do her daily shopping. I learned to tell a good cassava from a bad one, and how to bargain with the vendors. Those my mother didn't usually buy from would see me clutching my shopping list and think they could take advantage of my innocence. Instead I told them, "My mom always buys from that woman over there. So if you want me to buy from you today, you have to make the price better than hers."

The educational system at the time called for students who had completed their elementary school years to sit for an exam that would determine which secondary boarding school one could attend. Each student lists their top three choices, each of which must be in a different region in the country, and submit them to the West African Examination Council (WAEC) before taking the exam.

If a student's score is not good enough to qualify for their first choice, they are passed on to their second choice.

My parents preferred I go to a school in Accra, near home, and my teacher suggested the Presbyterian Boys secondary school, commonly know as Presec. It is a top-ranked boys school known for its emphasis on maths and science.

Another choice was the Achimota School, a coeducational boarding school also located in Accra. It boasted among its graduates three Ghanaian presidents and Robert Mugabe, the lifelong president of Zimbabwe. I would have been in good company attending either of those schools but I wanted to attend Prempeh College in Kumasi, capital of the Ashanti region, 150 miles from home.

I explained to my father, "I want to experience my Ashanti culture. I want to know your people. I want to go to the school that so many future doctors attended." I left out the fact that three of my best friends in elementary school had also selected Prempeh, my main reason for wanting to go there. But my teacher and my father prevailed and in filling out the application forms, my dad selected Presec as my first choice, Prempeh as my second, and Mfantispim, a school located on the coast, as my third.

He signed the forms and handed them to me to be submitted at school. I carried those forms around in my school bag for two days agonizing and scheming. Finally, I sat down with the forms and a razor blade and very carefully, with a pre-surgeon's steady hand and the determination of a ten-year-old, scraped off the top two selections. Then I replaced Presec with Prempeh, and vice versa.

My test scores were excellent and I was accepted by Prempeh. Although my father gave me an appropriate scolding, all was forgiven and I started my secondary school education far from home but with my friends. I was younger than most of the other new boys, and somewhat small for my age. One of the first teachers I encountered looked at me with raised eyebrows, shook her head, and exclaimed, "Why would any parent send their tiny little kid to a boarding school at your age?" I had no trouble with my studies or my classmates, and loved the adventure of living at school.

Prempeh College was founded in 1949 by the Ashanti king Sir Osei Tutu Agyeman Prempeh II and is considered the top secondary school in the country, modeled on Eton College in England. Like Eton boys, we all wore uniforms—dark green blazer, green shirt, green and yellow striped tie, and khaki shorts. Known for an emphasis on maths and sciences, Prempeh boasts the most graduates who have gone on to become physicians. It was the perfect place for me but a stretch for my parents to come up with the tuition and expenses, but each semester they somehow managed.

My seven years at Prempeh left a big impression on me. The days were highly regimented. We woke up at 5:30 each morning to do our chores—make up our beds for inspection, weed the gardens, water the flower beds, and sweep the hallways, dormitories, classrooms, and assembly hall.

If we were lucky and the tap water was running, we could get a quick shower. More often, we kids had to go fetch a bucket of water and bring it back to the dormitory. Water was the cause of many fights. A lower classman would lug his sloshing bucket of water all the way to the bathroom only to have a lazy upper-class bully take it away.

Hazing was an accepted part of boarding school culture and I suffered my share. My first year I slept on an upper bunk bed and a third-year student slept on the bottom. He was fond of waking me up after lights out to run errands for him. When I protested, he would order me to lie under his bed so that the springs were pressing down on me. I would wake up with the pattern of the springs etched into my cheeks.

Reporting him to the house master was out of the question. He was an alumnus who had gone through hazing himself. Besides, complaining was considered a sign of weakness. But one night nature handed me salvation. My bunk mate wet his bed. Squashed beneath his springs, I was baptized with the evidence. In the morning I let him know that unless he quit hazing me I would make sure everyone knew that he, a big, grown-up third-year student, was still wetting his bed. From then on I slept soundly in my upper bunk.

Prempeh was a prestigious school, but it was a school full of boys who welcomed a chance to express their idealism and independence. There had been growing discontent with the quality of the food, and some teachers were not showing up for their classes. Meanwhile, the headmaster, in the middle of a semester, announced that there would be extra fees to pay. A rumor began making the rounds that the headmaster was siphoning off school funds for his personal use.

When the student leaders presented their grievances, the headmaster responded in an odd and frightening way. First he ordered all 900 students to assemble outside the administration block, organized by class. Then a car drove onto the grounds and a handful of armed soldiers emerged.

The headmaster announced that a group of students had been caught smoking marijuana at the school stadium. Then, in groups of three or four, students were called out of line and interrogated by soldiers demanding that they point out any student they had ever seen smoking marijuana.

This process went on for hours. Perhaps the headmaster thought the spectacle would intimidate the student leadership from complaining. Instead, it emboldened them.

A mass demonstration was planned. We were to march into the town center to the mayor's office and then the palace of the Ashanti king. To preserve our moral position, no property was to be damaged. When the headmaster got wind of it, he warned that any student who participated would be expelled.

The students as a whole were undeterred, but I was one of the conflicted. I could not risk expulsion. With several hundred schoolmates in the crowd, I followed, chanting along with them our grievances. But when the mob reached the school gate, the boundary beyond which we had been warned would lead to expulsion, I turned back, as did a number of other students.

The demonstrators returned to campus about five hours later, shouting for the dismissal of the headmaster and in an ugly mood toward those of us who didn't go the distance. The punishment for our "cowardice" was a hazing called ponding, where a student is forcefully dumped in a dirty pond. In my case, the pond was overflowing with urine. It was an utterly humiliating experience but I felt I had no choice other than staying in bounds.

I had a much bigger goal for my life and I was not about to jeopardize it so casually. To the credit of the student leaders, the uprising achieved its goal and the headmaster was ousted.

In the British system, students complete their high

school requirements (first through fifth "forms") by the age of sixteen. They can take the "O Levels" (short for General Certificate of Education Ordinary Level exam) to qualify for sixth form (twelfth grade), roughly equivalent to the first two years of university. I passed my O Levels with excellent scores and made it to sixth form. It was a sign of achievement to get to wear the blue shirt and khaki pants of a sixth-former. A Prempeh graduate would then be eligible to apply directly to medical school without needing to earn a bachelor's degree first.

But first I had to take my A Level exams (short for General Certificate of Education Advanced Level). The A Level is offered through schools in the United Kingdom and British Crown dependencies to students completing secondary or pre-university education. Your score determines whether you can go on to university and what you can study.

The A Levels are rigorous and take place over three months. As I was studying for them I came down with malaria. Getting malaria in Ghana is like catching a cold, but this time it was a serious case, a cerebral type that is like encephalitis, affecting blood flow to the brain. It causes disorientation, losing track of time, and affects memory. All of these symptoms began to afflict me right before this big major exam.

I remember little of that feverish period except my aunties urging me to skip the exam. "Everybody will understand," they assured me. "You can take it the following year."

The disease had so scrambled my thoughts that I was convinced I had already taken the test. They kept trying to jog my memory and finally I grasped that the exams were going to be in a week. To move on with my class peers and remain competitive, I would have to sit for those exams, even though I had too little time to prepare and my brain was still recovering from its muddled state.

So I sallied forth and, for the first time in my academic career, scored poorly on a test. It had four parts and I got one B, one C, one D, and an E—not good enough to get into medical school, not good enough to qualify for scholarships abroad. It was a crushing blow that would end up being one of the best lessons I ever learned.

CHAPTER 3:
FROM COCONUTS
TO COSSACKS

"You know, we all understand," my mother told me. "As long as you did your best, something will happen and you will find a way."

She was right. I had already taken my Scholastic Aptitude tests (SATs) and the Test of English as a Foreign Language (TOEFL) and did well on both. Because of my unusual situation—recovering from malaria—I was able to retake the two A-Level tests I'd done so poorly in and got good marks that put me back on the medical school track.

That experience—bouncing back from a disappointment—was an important lesson and a turning point. I think of it as the victory that taught me to never give up my dreams. I had been motivated before, and now I began to push even harder.

My path to medical school included a detour. The 1979 coup had shut down the universities for a time and the entire educational system in Ghana stalled for a year. Once the schools reopened, to pick up the slack the government made it a requirement that sixth form graduates had to do a year of national service in the military or in community service. I wanted to spend my year working in a city hospital but that was one of the plum assignments that required political connections I didn't have. Instead I spent a year as a meteorological assistant, gathering and organizing weather data.

My first choice was to get my medical education in Kumasi at Kwame Nkrumah University of Science and Technology, named for Ghana's first president, the father of our independence. I submitted my application and also applied for scholarships to schools in the US, UK, and other European nations.

One of the first to show promise was the Early Medical Scholars program at the University of Rochester in New York, but they required a deposit of $160,000. In my provincialism, I couldn't imagine anyone having that kind of money. They must have assumed I was the son of a high official and my tuition would be subsidized, or the school just didn't do its homework. The average per capita annual income in Ghana at the time was about $400.

Where we lived at the time—a neighborhood of single-family houses, all walled with entrance gates—there were many in my age group attending Ghanaian boarding schools. During school holidays we often hung out, sharing stories about school, the latest movies we'd seen, plans for the future, and playing Scrabble, which was very popular.

Those who had families living in the US or London were the lucky ones. They would spend their summers abroad and return to school with stylish new wardrobes and the latest portable music player (the Walkman).

Whenever one of us got accepted to a school abroad—one that their families could afford—we all celebrated their success and were inspired to redouble our own efforts. One friend got a spot in a Swedish school and studied chemical engineering in Stockholm. Another went off to study civil engineering in Kiev, Ukraine.

My room filled with stacks of prospectuses and catalogs from colleges and medical schools around the world. A few wrote back offering financial aid, as much as 80 percent. But even the last 20 percent was out of our reach.

A large percentage of the schools I applied to were German and Swedish. Both governments encouraged international students by waiving all their expenses except for room and board, which I thought I could cover by working part time. Altogether I applied to a hundred or more medical schools and undergraduate colleges and competed for a number of scholarships.

My Kumasi application was still pending when I received notice that I'd won a good scholarship to a German medical school I fancied. I couldn't be certain I would be picked for one of only three dozen or so openings in Kumasi. But if I enrolled at the German school with a government-sponsored scholarship, I would no longer be eligible for the scholarship to Kwame Nkrumah University.

Studying abroad offered numerous advantages—more modern equipment and research, and more international opportunities—so I enrolled and withdrew from consideration in Kumasi. I took a German language course at the Goethe Institute while I waited for August to come around when I would be flying off to start my medical career. As part of the visa process I had to have a health screening after which I was told my passport and travel documents would come in the mail. When my passport arrived a few weeks later, I felt as though I was already on my way.

Ghana is a small country and in Accra and Kumasi, the two major cities with medical schools, all of those who intended to go into medicine knew who was going where and when. The days of August flew by but my paperwork did not arrive. Finally, in September, I ran into a friend who told me, "You know, the group that you are supposed to be going overseas with—I think they are gone already."

With my heart in my throat, I went to the government office where my travel and other documents were to be prepared and they confirmed what my friend had told me: "They are gone already." That's when I realized that somebody else had gotten my spot, someone with political connections, or more money to grease the wheels, and no one had bothered to tell me. The cruelty of it was hard to fathom. I had withdrawn my application from Kwame Nkrumah University, had my chance to study in Germany snatched away, and the semester had already begun, so it was probably too late to try to find a spot somewhere else. I made a rush trip to Kumasi to see if I could get a spot at the university but was told I was too late there also.

Soon after, I went to visit my maternal grandmother, who was nearly 90 years old and lived in a rural village near

Kumasi. She came with me on the drive back to Kumasi. The route took us past the main entrance to Nkrumah University. School had started and I could see through the entrance students carrying their books as they hurried to their classes. I stared with aching heart and flooding eyes at what could have been. It felt as though all my dreams were slipping through my fingers and I was helpless to stop it.

My grandmother had been watching me and after we passed the school she said something so wise that I remember it frequently, even today, as a turning point in my development and a touchstone during times of challenge.

"Son, don't be dejected by what has happened. What God has designed for you, nobody can take away."

This has come to define for me what is meant by faith. God has a plan, but He isn't ready to share it with me. Faith to me is the assurance of things hoped for and the conviction of things not seen. Another way of saying it might be that things happen for a reason, we just don't know what it is yet. In my youthful impatience, I believed I knew what path I ought to be on and could not comprehend why God seemed to be uncooperative.

Over time her words became a mantra, a reminder that has guided me through life when things haven't happened the way I wanted or thought they should. I still feel disappointment at times, but when I start to feel dejected I remember her words and trust that His design will reveal itself in time.

The window of opportunity had not quite shut. Ebenezer, a friend who lived two houses from ours and shared the same goal of gaining a scholarship to study abroad, had heard of a school in Sweden he thought was a good prospect and encouraged me to apply. He did the same, applying to study chemical engineering. We both were accepted with a scholarship. But to take advantage of this opportunity, I needed to get a visa.

There was no Swedish embassy in Ghana at the time and the nearest Swedish visa bureau was in Lagos, Nigeria, a city considered so dangerous my parents wouldn't let me go, even if I would have considered it.

Instead, I wrote to the Swedish school requesting documentation of my matriculation that would allow me to fly to Brussels, where I could go to the Swedish embassy to get the visa I needed to do my studies. It was a last-ditch effort to find a way around all the obstacles that seemed to keep popping up. I waited anxiously for a reply knowing that if it didn't come soon, or was rejected, there was only one remaining opportunity to start my medical education and that clock was ticking as well.

As compensation for the stolen opportunity to study in Germany, the government office in charge of scholarships offered me a chance to compete for a scholarship to study in the Soviet Union. One of my father's friends, a physician who was highly respected, had studied medicine in the Soviet Union. He encouraged me to pursue the opportunity and, after a series of exams and interviews, I was offered a full scholarship. But it included a detour of profound proportions: I would have to study veterinary medicine.

This was such deflating news. I had no interest in practicing veterinary medicine. But I reasoned that, as long as I was out of options, it couldn't hurt to learn about anatomy and disease in animals. As soon as I was able, I would reapply to the schools that would accept me for the study of human medicine. In the optimistic chance I would still have an opportunity to study in Germany, I continued studying German Language courses at the Goethe Institute.

While I was waiting to learn my academic fate, my brother George and I made cement blocks for a new house my father was building on a piece of land he owned. Each morning we mixed up a batch and poured it into forms. We could make up to about fifty a session. Then a truck carted them over to the site. We did this for months, until we had made the 3,000 or so necessary. I was glad to play a role in making one of my prayers come true, to see my parents safe in their own home again.

I held off giving my answer to the Soviet scholarship as long as I could. The day a group of Ghanaian students were to board a chartered plane for the flight to Moscow, I had to commit or risk losing even that chance. I could have passed up veterinary school and started the application process all over but that would have meant competing with a fresh crop of students, retaking exams, and, most important, it would be a loss of momentum. I was ready as I would ever be and eager to get started.

Finally, the day of the Moscow flight arrived—and no word from Sweden. My heart already heavy with the anticipation of saying goodbye to my family, knowing I might not see them for many years, I put my bag in the car and struck out for the airport with my parents in August 1990. In my pocket was about fifty dollars that my old Nana had given me during my last visit. When I told her it looked like I would be going to Russia, she pulled a book from a shelf in her tiny room, opened it, and took out some currency.

"I don't have much, but this is what I have for you, and whatever it can do to help you in your travels, take it." It was a deeply moving experience, knowing that she had saved that money over many years and was trusting me to use it wisely. I sensed this would likely be the last time we would speak.

On the way to the airport, we made one final stop at the post office to see if there might be the letter that would stay my execution, but there was none. So, after a tearful farewell, I followed the other students onto the plane, a young man about to begin the first leg of my career in a cold, remote place I hadn't chosen, to live among people who had a reputation for being hostile to Africans, to study a specialty I wasn't interested in and never intended to practice, leaving my family and

everything familiar behind. I sometimes wonder what path I might have chosen had I known it would be nearly a decade before I would again feel my mother's embrace.

The day after I left, my father picked up the mail, including a letter informing me that my precious Swedish documents would be waiting for me at the embassy in Brussels, where they would eventually expire unclaimed.

Twenty years old, dressed and ready to leave home on the day I departed for Moscow in 1990, holding my baby sister, Yvette.

CHAPTER 4:
LOST IN TRANSLATION

My medical career began in a hospital, but not as a student and not voluntarily.

For my first-year studies I had been assigned to attend a university in Krasnodar, a city of about 600,000 in Russia's far south, near the Black Sea, just east of the Crimean Peninsula. Up until that point my interest in world affairs had revolved around international soccer, music, and academics. Now I was to have a ringside seat at one of the most significant events of the late twentieth century—the breakup of the Soviet Union and the emergence of modern Russia.

The relationship between the Soviet Union and Africans began with the liberal granting of educational scholarships for study in the best universities in Russia. It was part of the Cold War strategy to offset alliances between former colonies and the NATO nations. Once out from under foreign rule, the Soviets recruited a large contingent of students—an estimated

400,000 over four decades—to study medicine, engineering, and agronomy. Across Africa, many of these Soviet graduates became respected leaders on the continent, exactly what the program was intended to do—create allies.

My focus was on achieving my educational goals, hopefully without being sidetracked by rapidly evolving geopolitical events. Nevertheless, before leaving Ghana I visited the Russian cultural office in Accra and learned the Cyrillic letters and a bit about Russian culture, as well as the meaning of perestroika (rebuilding)—the name given to the reform movement—and glasnost (openness)—the term used to describe the new policy.

My first ride in an airplane was a thrill, and long. Too wound up to sleep, I arrived with my fellow students exhausted after the twelve-hour flight and surrendered to deep sleep at the Moscow

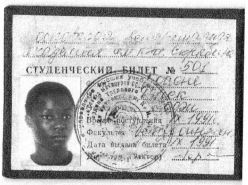

My Russian student identity card.

hotel we had been driven to directly from the Sheremetyevo airport, with a stern warning not to leave.

The next morning a consular officer from the Ghana embassy came to welcome us, followed by some stern-faced women in white lab coats who drew blood for various tests including malaria and HIV, which was becoming epidemic in much of Africa. We were instructed not to leave the hotel until the results came back, after which we were sent off to our various destinations in the Soviet Union.

Some students ended up in the Baltic States, others in Ukraine, some in St. Petersburg, and I was assigned to go to the city of Krasnodar in southern Russia to begin my preveterinary studies. It would prove to be a fortuitous assignment because Krasnodar is an agricultural center with an abundance of food whereas most of the rest of the disintegrating Soviet Union was experiencing shortages.

A week or so after I arrived in Krasnodar, I was sitting in a classroom with other students during an orientation session when I heard my name being called out. "Mr. Boahene!" A man in a uniform at the door motioned me to follow him.

A moment later I found myself outside on the street being ordered into the back of a windowless ambulance. The doors of the patient compartment slammed shut and the vehicle lurched into motion for a terrifying ride to—where? The driver and his companion sat in the front and even if I could have talked to them, I was not yet able to communicate in Russian. After a short, bumpy ride, the vehicle stopped. A moment later the back doors swung open in front of a hospital.

I was hustled inside to a unit with an open ward filled with beds. In the corner was an isolation room into which I was ushered and given hospital pajamas and flip-flops to change into. Then my street clothes were whisked away and the door closed.

It looked just like a prison cell—bare walls painted a dull institutional green with patches where there had been water damage or paint had flaked off. A grimy window looked out onto an interior shaft. The only furniture was a squeaky steel-spring bed with a thin mattress on top. I sat and tried to figure out what had just happened. Nothing made sense. Surely there had been a colossal bureaucratic mistake and someone from the school would walk through the door any minute now and sort it all out so I could get back to orientation.

Instead, the next person through the door was an orderly bringing me some bread and a bowl of what I presumed to be soup—a clear broth with a few slices of cabbage. Traditional Ghanaian soup is a blend of exotic ingredients including okra, tomatoes, pepper, eggplant, and a variety of spices. My favorite is peanut butter soup. This was about as appetizing as lukewarm dishwater. I nibbled some of the bread, laid down, and eventually drifted off into a fitful sleep.

The next morning a nurse showed up and, without a word or a smile, stuck me with a needle and took a blood sample. I tried to communicate the "why" question, holding my hands out in supplication. But she went about her work methodically and without so much as a glance. The German I so diligently studied in Accra—thinking I would end up studying there—was of no use. The color of my skin made me feel particularly isolated. Black faces in Russia, especially outside of Moscow, were rare. All that day my attempts to engage the nurses and orderlies by smiling were greeted with cold stares.

The next day passed like the first, and the next and the next. The room was utterly depressing, especially for someone who was healthy, as far as I knew, and used to tropical conditions. The air was often foul with the smell of feces and disinfectant.

This became my life and routine for nearly three weeks. If I was sick, why was I not being given any medicine? The older nurses were strict and grim. I was not to leave the room and when I dared try, they immediately ordered me back inside. I came to despise the phrase, "Go to your room," and still do.

The Russia I arrived in had just that summer become a sovereign state after nearly seven decades as part of the Soviet Union. The Berlin Wall had come down less than a year earlier. A revolutionary conflict was going on in the government between former Soviet hardliners and reformers. The Russian economy was stalling and the incidence of diseases like diphtheria and measles was rising, on the way to epidemic levels.

Looking back at photos taken of Russian life around that time—1990 to 1993—it is nearly impossible to find a single smiling or laughing face, with good reason. Money was scarce, prices were rising, and a civil war seemed inevitable. I had followed the news and expected to be challenged, but as a young, aspiring African raised in a generally optimistic society, the culture shock and unfamiliar climate were overwhelming. Now, on top of all that, I was being held like a prisoner.

The younger nurses were curious and friendlier. When the senior staff was off duty they left my door open, allowing them to peek in now and then and allowing me to sneak out and roam a bit. In the process I met a Russian teenager named Aleksei, also a patient. He spoke some English and was naturally curious, so we quickly become friends.

At night when my door was left open Aleksei would visit and we'd chat. Sometimes the younger nurses would join us. He taught me some Russian phrases and I taught him the counterparts in English.

When Aleksei was discharged—I never learned why he was there—the sense of isolation became intense. My spirits sank lower each day as the nurses took blood samples without explanation. Russian hospital food disagreed with all my senses—tasteless boiled potatoes, gristly meats in greasy sauces, rank-smelling cabbage, and beet soup the color of oxblood.

I was worried about missing my classes, thinking about home and family, and praying. I found a bit of respite when I discovered that early in the mornings, before the senior nurses came on their rounds to draw blood, I could escape the ward and the hospital and go outside for a walk. The first day I walked out of the building was exhilarating. I was an escapee so every time I heard a siren I expected an ambulance to come racing around the corner to capture me.

When I'd been kidnapped from school I'd had a few rubles with me, so I went looking for something I could eat. I found a shop where I was able to buy some rice and some ice cream—Heaven! Unable to decode prices, I handed the cashier a five ruble note, about $8.00 at the prevailing exchange rate. She picked up an abacus, a mechanical calculator that dates back several centuries, and began flicking brown and black beads until she finally gave me my change.

This became my routine for a number of days. When I wasn't looking for food, I loitered in shops just to be out of the dreary ward. Instead I had to endure the stares of customers and clerks. Most Russians had never seen an African in person, and here was one wearing pajamas and slippers in public. I'm sure they assumed that was the way we dressed back home.

After two or three weeks stuck in this state of suspended animation, I became so despondent I contemplated trying to contact the Ghana consulate and demanding to be sent home. But I had no way to find out how to do that.

Deliverance came after three weeks of quarantine. An older woman doctor came on rotation and I discovered she spoke German. I had studied German in Accra so all of my pent-up frustration came tumbling out. I demanded she contact the Ghana embassy in Moscow to let them know where I was and my wish to be sent back to Ghana.

She was sympathetic and promised my ordeal would be over soon. I insisted she write a discharge note in my diary. She kept her word and I was driven back to the hostel to rejoin my schoolmates who had assumed I was lost for good.

It would be nearly a year before I found out why it happened, and only then by accident. I was visiting the student medical center for neck pain and happened to notice that my medical chart was rather thick for someone who'd had no problems. While the nurse was distracted I leafed through the pages. I scanned the Cyrillic lettering—a language I now understood—and a key phrase popped out: "... quarantined for risk of malaria parasites." There was a series of check-boxes, all with marks in the "none" column. I shudder to think how long I would have been stuck there had that German-speaking doctor not come along.

At the end of my hospital ordeal I was relieved to discover that my classmates had only been studying Russian. I had not missed any of the academic classes and having spent nearly a month immersed in the language, I was actually ahead of the class. Back in my university dorm, I quickly adapted and joined the small community of African students who tended to study, cook, and socialize together to stave off homesickness.

The worst bout for me came early, when I received my first letter from home. The news included the unexpected death of a beloved uncle and my heart felt like it would break from yearning to be home, mourning with my family.

On the other end, my poor parents—watching scenes of long lines for food and of political violence in Moscow—tried sending me food. They would put together a package of non-perishables and my father would drive to the airport when flights to Moscow were scheduled to leave, finding travelers who would agree to mail it when they arrived.

The address my parents had for me was in Moscow, not Krasnodar. So those packages ended up in the hands of other students who were hungrier than I and thoughtful enough to call and let me know how much they appreciated it. Food was not a problem in Krasnodar so to reassure my parents and relieve them of the burden of trying to feed me from afar, I sent them a photo showing them my chubby cheeks.

"As you can see," I wrote, "I am fat and happy."

CHAPTER 5:
COSSACKS TO
KLAN COUNTRY

My first-year class included students who were going to study human medicine as well as those of us headed to veterinary school. We all studied the same basic sciences—general chemistry, biology, physics, and related subjects. I had taken many of these courses in Ghana, but now had to learn the material in a new language, a challenge but ultimately rewarding.

My language teacher, Ludmila Vasilievna, was a middle-aged woman with a motherly manner who made us foreign students feel at home. Hers was the only Russian home I visited during my time there. She went out of her way after I returned from quarantine to give me extra lessons to help me catch up to the other students.

I also studied Russian literature and philosophy as well as Latin. The philosophy class was my least favorite as it was a dogmatic depiction of Russia's role in the world as opposed to an exploration of creativity and ideas by its major thinkers.

I enjoyed Russian literature and was exposed for the first time to the works of Pushkin and Tolstoi. I memorized a few poems including Pushkin's well known 1829 love poem, "Я вас любил.../I loved you once."

Я вас любил: любовь еще, быть может
В душе моей угасла не совсем;
Но пусть она вас больше не тревожит;
Я не хочу печалить вас ничем.
Я вас любил безмолвно, безнадежно,
То робостью, то ревностью томим;
Я вас любил так искренно, так нежно,
Как дай вам бог любимой быть другим.

I loved you once: perhaps that love has yet
To die down thoroughly within my soul;
But let it not dismay you any longer;
I have no wish to cause you any sorrow.
I loved you wordlessly, without a hope,
By shyness tortured, or by jealousy.
I loved you with such tenderness and candor
And pray God grants you to be loved that way again.

Russian became my fourth language fluency after Ashanti, English, and German. I was becoming a man of the world

I studied hard, hoping that if I kept my marks high the

people in charge would let me switch from vet to med school. For the moment, however, my aim was to be in Moscow, an international capital with a population of about nine million where I would have access to resources I would need, like central government offices and foreign embassies. Krasnodar's population was about 600,000. It is the regional capital in a border area with Georgia and Ukraine and was in flux at the time, a destination for a flood of refugees.

In the end I was told I couldn't switch no matter how good my marks, but the school I was being assigned to, the State Academy of Veterinary Medicine and Biotechnology of K.I. Scriabin in Moscow, was considered harder to get into than Russian medical schools. I was disappointed but undeterred, motivated by something my father took time to speak to me about before I left home. I am shy by nature and he explained that there would be times when I must be more assertive to get what I wanted. I would have to make my own case. I knew how, and I boarded the plane to leave Krasnodar bound for Moscow prepared to do just that.

Straight from Moscow's Domodedovo Airport I found my way by metro to the national Ministry of Education and Health offices where I presented myself at reception, informing the reception clerk that I needed to see the minister. He didn't smile but there was the hint of a smirk.

"You need an appointment."

"No. I insist on seeing him today. It's very important."

I hectored and charmed and explained until he capitulated and placed a phone call. Finally I got to speak to a deputy minister, who remarked on my determination and courage but told me, "Why don't you just continue the full year of school and then we'll see." Thus, after my initial year of studying prerequisites in Krasnodar, Moscow became my new home.

One of the first courses you take in medical school, be it human or veterinary medicine, is gross anatomy. This is when students first learn about the different parts of bodies by dissecting one. In medical school you work on cadavers of humans. I had done animal dissections in high school of small animals like frogs, rabbits, fish, and so on. My first dissection in veterinary school was on a horse—an impressive specimen. Just as in human dissections, the students worked in teams on a carcass that was kept submerged in a tank of formaldehyde.

When we were ready to begin, wearing masks against the searing odor and aprons to protect our street clothes, the push of a button started a crane that would lift the horse up out of the tank and set it on a huge table. We would then take turns with scalpels separating the various muscles, nerves, blood vessels, and other structures. One student would read the dissection instructions from a book while the rest took turns either dissecting or watching and taking notes.

When I finally got to medical school much later, I realized that veterinary medicine is in fact a more complex discipline because there are so many different species and so many different sizes. After the horse we dissected a cow and a dog. I also took a course called zoo engineering where we observed one of the anatomy professors go through a prosection (review of a previously dissected specimen) of a Siberian tiger.

There are many similarities between the human and animal anatomies and the use of Latin-based nomenclature helps when discussing different species. Diseases in animals are also similar to those in humans—cancers, fractures, and influenza, for example. What I was learning would prove to be helpful when I finally did get to medical school.

Among my friends at home I had been known as Egg, as in egghead—with my nose always in a book and always striving for the best grade. I was just as conscientious and competitive in Moscow, and welcomed opportunities to hone my skills in non-academic activities, winning a first-place award in a Russian quiz bowl for exchange students.

I also became known for my temperance and the faith that sustains it. Many of the international students, including Africans, were quite taken with Russian culture, especially the drinking. A lot of students drank regularly and there was catting around as well. It was easy for foreign students to attract the most beautiful and brilliantly smart Russian girls. They practically threw themselves at us in part because we were exotic and no doubt because we held the possibility of emigrating to a more stable and prosperous country where their careers would have a better chance of flourishing. The majority of my friends had affairs and many ended up marrying Russians, including Ghanaians.

My friends once tried to set me up with a computer lecturer, a very beautiful woman who they assured me was interested. "Don't you realize? She really, really likes you. What are you going to do about it?"

"What is there to do?"

My parents had raised my siblings and I to avoid alcohol and to remain chaste until marriage. I didn't drink and had no desire to start. I had also made a commitment to remain celibate while single. My friends, many of whom indulged themselves, teased me, making bets among themselves on how long it would take before I picked up drinking and had a Russian girlfriend.

I just smiled and assured them, "You will be waiting a long time."

It wasn't enough to hold strong beliefs. Just minding your own business could get foreign students into a world of trouble. One evening I went to visit a friend who was a medical student at the Peoples' Friendship University in Moscow, a Cold War–inspired institution specifically for students from developing nations in Asia, Africa, and South America. It was well known as a magnet for Russian girls hoping to meet up with foreign men. But it was also a magnet for Russian hooligans looking for foreigners to beat up for—among other transgressions—fraternizing with Russian girls. Africans were the most frequent targets.

As I knocked on the door of my friend's apartment I could hear loud music inside. After several attempts to get someone's attention, I gave up and turned to walk away when I was confronted by a skimpily dressed Russian girl reeking of alcohol. She blocked my escape and invited me to go with her to a party. When I made it clear I wasn't interested, she grabbed a handful of my shirt and threatened to scream for help, as if I had made an unwanted advance.

This was a well-known scheme to shake down students for money or other favors, and it was effective because the police would never side with an African student over a Russian. We foreigners all knew of students who had ended up in jail after being falsely accused or, even worse, got stomped by Russian boys who always seemed to be loitering around campus looking to start trouble. I pushed her out of my way and raced as fast as I could back to my dorm, feeling like I had just dodged a bullet.

The social life I enjoyed most was getting to know students from other African countries like Tunisia, Ethiopia, and South Africa. There were also students from Europe and Latin America and it was entertainment enough just exchanging stories and sharing languages, music, and customs.

Travel was my other passion. Whenever school was out, I bought a train ticket and visited a new city, or travelled to other countries. In the smaller Russian cities where people had never seen a black person, when I went for a walk everyone stared. In Moscow there were enough Africans that there wasn't as much staring, but xenophobia was simmering just below the surface. It was expressed in many ways but particularly in resentment by ordinary Russians—who'd struggled for decades under an oppressive and secretive government—about certain privileges enjoyed by foreigners.

Before the dissolution of the Soviet Union, it was difficult for ordinary Russians to get visas to travel abroad whereas students like myself could simply phone an embassy, set up an appointment, and get one without a wait. As a citizen of Ghana, a Commonwealth nation, there were no obstacles to getting visas to visit the UK, for example.

Although the ban on Russians traveling abroad was dropped, for Russians to get an exit visa was hard, required a great deal of patience, and there were often bribes involved. It was common to go to an embassy for a popular destination and find hundreds of Russians waiting in line. That's what happened when some friends and I wanted to travel to Germany during a school break. Each of us took turns waiting in a line over two days and two nights.

During one of my turns in line, a Russian man walked up to me, squinted, reached up with his hand, and ran the tip of his index finger across my cheek. Then he examined it, turned to someone behind him, and declared in a booming voice, "I told you it wouldn't rub off."

The other fellow chuckled nervously and there were titters up and down the line. It was so strange that I was confused at first, but then it hit me that he was having fun at my expense. I began to scold him, quite loudly for me, in perfect Russian. His face flushed as some of the other Russians in the queue came to his defense.

"Young man, he's just a country farmer—never traveled, never seen anything."

"He doesn't know any better."

I was incensed. "He can still read. He should know these things."

That was a mild example of the prejudice that had begun to percolate in the post-Soviet period. The old order was breaking down and certain inhibitions seemed to be fading. Africans, including some of the students I knew, were taunted and in some cases beaten up. Later some were even murdered by street thugs. Foreigners in general were being targeted by thieves who stole with impunity knowing the police would ignore the complaints of the victims.

Russians particularly resented foreigners who could take advantage of our travel visas by buying goods abroad that we could bring back and sell at a profit. Blue jeans were popular and easy to sell in the newly deregulated economy. Entrepreneurial storeowners with empty store shelves were eager for foreign goods. Since I couldn't work in Russia, it was one way I might make the money I needed to cover the gap between living expenses and the small stipends I got from the Russian and Ghanaian governments. I was also determined to accumulate a nest egg to fall back on or use to move on after vet school. I approached several storeowners and got a list of items they were interested in selling.

First, however, I tried to get a ticket on the Trans-Siberian Express that linked Moscow with Beijing via Vladivostok. It was a popular route and sounded like a great adventure but was impossible to book. I decided instead to visit Turkey, a train journey of almost four days requiring a Soviet exit visa to guarantee I would be allowed to re-enter, visas for Bulgaria and Turkey, and confusion about whether visas were required for passage through the newly independent Ukraine. For Russians, the shock of all these changes included finding out that relatives who lived in Ukraine and Belarus were no longer citizens of the same country.

In addition to the $50 my grandmother had given me when I left home, I had saved $100 from my monthly stipend. That $150 was not much to start a trans-European business so I invited some friends to invest with me to increase my working capital. Two other students joined me on the trip, one from Ghana and from Ethiopia.

During a long stopover to change trains in Bucharest, Romania, I was in a restaurant buying some food when I felt a bump from behind. Turning around, I caught a young man just as he was dipping his hand into my back pocket where I had been carrying my passport.

My loud complaints scared him off before he could get a grip. Had I lost my passport, getting back to Moscow would have become a huge problem. This was especially true in Bucharest, a city that had attracted a large number of African refugees hoping to reach Western Europe where they could start new lives.

Passports stolen from young Africans studying in the Soviet Union could be sold to stranded African immigrants in Bucharest for thousands of dollars because Caucasian immigration officers had trouble telling us apart. My close call with a document disaster gave me quite a scare when I realized the terrible stateless situation in which those young men were trapped.

Later, I was approached by a group of young Africans I overheard speaking Ashanti, saying, "This one looks like a Ghanaian." I ignored their attempts to speak to me. The incident made me more determined than ever to avoid any chance I might end up like them.

Once we arrived in Istanbul I headed straight for the Grand Bazaar, a huge covered market that is the world's top tourist destination. It might have been intimidating had I not had so much experience bargaining with vendors as a child for my mother, and later in the largest single market in West Africa, the Kejetia (Central) Market in Kumasi, where I attended boarding school.

My shopping list included leather jackets, Western jeans, blouses, T-shirts, and men's dress shoes. I bought and packed two bulging suitcases that I lugged the four-day journey back to Moscow. I sold all of it in one day, earned a good profit, and returned my investors' money with interest.

Late that first summer break I traveled to Germany to visit one of my Prempeh schoolmates who was studying medicine at the University of Ulm. Western Germany was everything Russia was not. Shops were filled with goods, the streets were immaculate, and the whole country seemed to have a bright outlook. People smiled in Germany and being black was not a big deal. Germans had become used to foreigners since the end of World War Two, especially Americans in uniform, including many who were African American.

Ulm was one of the schools I had applied to but failed to win a spot at, so visiting left me in a slightly melancholy mood on the train back to Moscow, a young and eager man contemplating what might have been as though it were a loss. Years later, quite a bit wiser, I would recall that visit with a heightened appreciation of God's plan for me when I returned to Germany, this time as a visiting US professor from a prestigious institution coming to teach residents and other surgeons and to perform complex facial surgeries.

My veterinary school tuition was covered by a generous Russian government scholarship that I discovered one day had strings attached when I was summoned to the university president's office. He was there to greet me, along with a group of senior students and faculty advisers. They asked me how my experience had been so far and complimented me on my excellent marks. They said I was doing so well and was such a model student that they wanted to put me on the student council.

From older students I had heard that those who sat on the council were expected to spy on other students. In exchange, council members got to have their own furnished apartments instead of sharing four-up like the rest of us. The one African student I knew who was on the student council and had his own apartment was shunned by the African community. When they couldn't avoid his company, they were careful about what they said.

I couldn't accept the offer but I was afraid that declining outright might be taken as an insult. So I kicked the can down the road.

"I'm so glad that you think highly of me, but I'm very busy just now getting ready for World International Day."

That was the school's annual cultural event and it was a big deal. Foreign student groups put on costumes and performed indigenous music and dance pieces for dignitaries and party officials. It was true that I was involved in preparing the Ghanaian presentation, so it was a good cover story. "Once International Day is over, I can consider it."

That seemed to satisfy everyone and I walked out of the president's office somewhat thunderstruck by my dilemma. I was about halfway through the program, but I didn't want to get entangled in politics. I was certain that if I agreed to sit on the student council but refused to spy, I'd probably face some manufactured impediments. Either way, I would have to leave and I didn't want to go back to Ghana with a half-finished degree and no prospects for medical school. Where could I go?

After I left Ghana my younger sister Elaine won a scholarship to attend Chatham Hall, a girls' private boarding secondary school in Chatham, Virginia. For her to accept an invitation to go to the home of a classmate over a weekend or holiday the school had to call my parents in Ghana for permission. International calls were unreliable so sometimes my sister had to stay at school while everyone else left. My parents decided to find her a host family that could take her in on holidays and give her the permissions she needed to visit friends on the weekends. They found a family through my father's missionary network.

My plan was to visit my sister at her host family's home and then, while I was in America, try to find a university or medical school that would have me. However, the word among my fellow students was that the US was not giving visas to any foreign students in Moscow because most of them just stayed in the States, living and working illegally. So when I told my friends I was going to go to the US embassy to get a visa, they just laughed.

"Don't waste your time. A lot of people have tried and they never got one."

"I'm not a lot of people," I said. "I'm going to get it."

It was a risky move because visa refusals were stamped in your passport. Once your passport had been so stamped, it made it very hard to get a visa to go anywhere else. It was a black mark that other countries took notice of, even friendly nations like Germany.

"God has a plan for you." My grandmother's words returned to me as I prayed the night before my interview. I prayed that His plan included getting that visa. I gave myself a pep talk of my father's advice. Be assertive. Make your own case.

To prove I had the means to come back, I took with me about 1,000 British pounds I had saved from selling jeans and from working as a school janitor during holiday visits to London. I also took the address and phone of my sister's host family, and of her school.

The visa clerk was young, maybe a year or two out of college. That made me hopeful and feel a bit more assertive. We were peers and maybe he had not been doing his job long enough to become jaded and cynical.

He began taking down my information, ticking off a checklist of questions.

"Do you have any money?"

I showed him the wad of British bank notes.

"Is all of that actually your money? You didn't borrow it to show it to me, did you?"

"Yes, it's all mine."

"What do your parents do?"

"My father is a truck driver. My mum is a bank teller."

"What's the purpose of your visit?"

"To see my sister."

"What does she do?"

"She's in school."

"Which school?"

"Chatham Hall. It's in Virginia."

He looked up, squinted, and cocked his head.

"Chatham Hall? Are you sure?"

"Yes, that's where she is."

"Well, who pays her tuition?"

"She's on scholarship."

He asked for the school's number, picked up his telephone receiver and dialed it straight away. A minute later he was talking to someone at Chatham Hall who confirmed that, yes, my sister is enrolled in good standing, and yes, she is a scholarship student, and yes, she has a brother named Derek (my anglicized name) in Moscow.

"Okay," he said, hanging up. "Now, when you go, where are you going to stay?"

"With my sister's host family in Ar ... Ark ... Kansas."

He squinted again. "Where?"

I looked at the address in my papers and read it aloud. "Harrison, Ark ... Ark Kansas."

"You mean Arkansas, the state. Have you ever been there?"

"No."

"Okay, what's the name of the family you're going to go stay with? Do you have their phone number?"

He dialed as I read it out.

"Is this the Lennon residence? ... Cindy? ... Are you Mrs. Lennon? ... This is the US embassy visa section in Moscow and I have a young man from Ghana here with me who says he'll be visiting you and I was wondering if you wouldn't mind .... "

From across his desk I could hear what sounded like a woman screaming.

"Yes, ma'am, that's good. Yes, well I ... Yes ... Of course, if ... . Uh-huh. That's fine, so ... "

It took him a long time to get Cindy off the phone, and when he finally hung up he made a whistling sound.

"Geez! Those people really want you to go, don't they? So your dad's a missionary, huh?"

Then came the hardest question, the one that would make or break my case.

"Okay, so prove to me that when you leave you're not going to just stay there. How do I know you're going to come back?"

There is no easy answer to a question like that. How do

you prove a negative? But I had thought it through the night before so I was prepared.

"You seem to be about my age or maybe a year or two older, so you probably graduated from college not so long ago and then you were posted to Moscow, right?"

He leaned back in his chair and nodded. "Yeah, that's about right."

"So when you're done with your service here, do you want to go back to the States?"

"Yes, I most definitely do."

"Well, I'm not Russian, and I'm not an American. I'm on a full scholarship, studying veterinary medicine. It's a very competitive field. I'm from a poor country and this is a great opportunity. Why would I go anywhere else and give it up?"

He nodded.

"If I went to America with the idea of not coming back, what would I do there? If I had been accepted at a school, admitted to a veterinary school, then yes. I would not be coming back. But if I go without any such option, why would I stay and sacrifice my hard work? Of course, I would come back and finish my degree and I think you would do the same."

He clicked his pen a few times as he regarded me in silence.

Then he abruptly sat back up and began to write. "Can you stick around to pick up your visa today?"

I fought to keep a sober face. "Yes, of course."

"Okay, then. Come back after lunch and it'll be ready."

I floated out the door and into the street, wanting to cry, laugh, and shout all at once.

When I returned to school I put my passport away in a secure place, laid on my bed, and pretended to sleep. When my roommates came home I heard one of them say, "Don't bother him. He's really sad. They refused him the visa." I wanted to savor my victory by myself a little longer and enjoy the looks on their faces when I revealed the truth.

I managed to keep it to myself for the rest of that day. The next morning when everyone was up, I did my best to pull a long face and casually showed one of my roommates my passport, opened to the page with the visa stamp.

"Kofi! But … but … How in the world did you do that?"

"You just have to tell them the truth." Everything I had said was true. Why would I give up what I had invested so much in? It was also true that if I had the opportunity to stay, I would probably seize it. But it was equally true that I would not stay in the States illegally, which was really the question he asked. I had decided that I did not want to have to live off the grid and end up driving a taxi and dodging the immigration service. If I were to have a legitimate career in medicine, I would have to figure out how to do it legitimately.

It was true that I would have wanted to finish veterinary school, but the situation in Russia was starting to spiral out of control. There was an attempted coup against Premier Gorbachev while I was visiting friends in Germany. I was about to return to Moscow when my schoolmates called to warn me. "It's not safe. Don't come back yet."

I waited a few weeks and returned to finish one more semester. The situation continued to deteriorate. There were military vehicles all over Moscow yet it was unsafe for any foreign students to venture far from school. My plan was to go to London and work during the 1992 summer holiday to save some extra money, and then go to the States to visit my sister and her American host family. Then I could investigate whether a legal way could be found to stay and continue my studies.

I packed my bags with everything I thought I'd need or didn't want to leave behind. When I got to the border the authorities refused to let me through. The inspectors found a pair of binoculars in my suitcase and decided I was a suspicious person.

"There's nothing to it," I pleaded. "You guys can keep them. Just let me go."

They wouldn't yield and I missed my train, losing the price of an expensive ticket. I was desperate. If I didn't leave soon I might become a target for a racist attack. Meanwhile, the Russian government was going broke. If I had to stay, my scholarship and stipend could be at risk. I would probably have been prohibited from going anywhere except back home to Ghana.

So I bought a ticket to the nearest destination in Poland, put all my belongings in a storage locker at the train station on the Russian side, and with my passport, wallet, some money, and the clothes I was wearing, returned to the border at Bryansk where the guards, lacking an excuse to turn me away, let me pass. From Warsaw I flew to London and, after working for a couple of months to raise more money, flew from London to Dallas, Texas, where I went to the American Airlines counter to buy my ticket to my final destination.

The ticket agent behind the counter looked at me quizzically. "Where?"

"Harrison, Ar …kansas." I was still having trouble pronouncing it.

"Honey," she said, "Are you sure you have the right name? Is that where you really want to go?"

"Yes." I showed her the written address for Cindy Lennon.

"Hold on a sec." She huddled with another agent. Then they both came over and the supervisor asked me the same question.

"Good morning, sir," he said. "We just wanted to make sure you're getting on the right plane. Harrison, Arkansas. Is that really where you want to go?"

I assured them it was, but the repeated questioning, in Moscow and now in Dallas, was worrisome.

"Sweetheart," the woman said. "What on earth are you gonna do there?"

CHAPTER 6:
ARE WE IN THE WRONG PLACE?

Cindy Lennon became a pen pal of my father's in 1989, a year or so before I left Ghana for Russia. An American pastor she knew had been on an African mission trip and made a stop in Accra that included a visit to my father's congregation. This pastor had been moved by my father's words and recorded a couple of his sermons which he shared later with Cindy when he got back home.

Cindy was in elementary school when she developed a fascination with African culture and the struggles of its peoples from reading *National Geographic* magazine articles. She dreamt of going one day.

In one of my father's sermons that she listened to he mentioned wanting to have a pen pal in the States. So Cindy sat down and wrote him a letter that launched a correspondence lasting a quarter-century, so far.

About the time I left home, my sister Elaine had won a scholarship to Chatham Hall, a century-old private girls' boarding school in Chatham, Virginia, whose alumni include the noted artist Georgia O'Keefe. When the issue came up of who might be her guardian while she was in the States, to handle travel permissions and emergencies, my father wrote to Cindy asking her to "please take care of my daughter."

Cindy and her husband, Joe, lived at the time in Clarksdale, Mississippi, where Joe worked for a department store chain. Clarksdale is in an agricultural region of the Deep South with a population of 17,000 or so that is eighty percent black, with nearly half the residents living below the official poverty level. However, the town has the distinction of being one of the incubators of the Mississippi Blues music movement of the 1920s and 1930s. The musician Sam Cooke was born in Clarksdale and the town today is the home of the Delta Blues Museum.

Moving there had been a big culture shock for the Lennons, who had lived for many years in a predominantly white middle-class neighborhood in Alabama. It was Cindy's first experience being in the vast minority and rubbing shoulders with black people on a daily basis.

At first she was uncomfortable. "I found prejudices in myself that I didn't know were there," she said later. "But looking back, it was so perfect, and a good place to live."

The Lennons were a natural fit as a host family. Their eldest son had recently graduated from high school and was in the Army, and they had a twelve-year-old still living at home. Joe's job had allowed Cindy to be a full-time mother and homemaker.

So Cindy and Joe agreed to stand in as parents, although Cindy chuckled over my father's apparent geographical myopia. The drive from the school to Clarksdale is more than twelve hours. As it happened, or was destined to be, one of the Chatham teachers was from Jackson, Mississippi. On her spring break, Elaine rode down to Jackson with her teacher and Cindy made the two-hour drive down from Clarksdale to meet her.

Cindy remembers, "I thought Elaine was going to knock me over. She just ran to me and hugged me so hard. We'd never met, but she already considered me her American mother. I was deeply touched and felt an immediate bond." That instant bond is a characteristic of Ghanaian culture where extended families of relatives and friends are common.

Cindy and her family learned firsthand the truth in the proverb that a stream never forgets its source. They noticed at meals that Elaine would hardly eat. Cindy asked if she was all right, or if she didn't like the food and wanted something else. Why wasn't a healthy young woman eating?

It took a bit of wheedling to get Elaine to confess with downcast eyes, "I can't eat when I know my family doesn't have enough." This is an emotion I have felt myself. Sitting at a bounteous table feels almost disloyal when you know your loved ones are struggling to keep everyone's stomach full.

When Cindy was able to speak, wiping away a tear, she told Elaine what my sister needed to hear. "It's not going to help them for you to make yourself sick." That seemed to do the trick. Elaine started eating normally.

By 1992, when I escaped to London via Poland with my passport and little else, and when I was ready to use my American visa, the Lennons had moved from Mississippi to Harrison, Arkansas. It's a county seat (courts and government offices) with a population of just over 10,000, ninety-seven percent of them white. It was another culture shock, from living among black people to rarely seeing any. Cindy remembers looking around and thinking, "Are we in the wrong place? God, what are you doing? What are you preparing us for?"

So Cindy worried a bit when the telephone rang one day and it was me, calling from London, telling the Lennons (in an accent that required me to repeat everything two or three times) that I was ready to make the leap. Cindy wondered how big a problem the color of my skin might be in a town associated with the most virulently racist group in America, the Ku Klux Klan.

I was oblivious to all that. I had few preconceived ideas about what it would be like in the States. Because of its colonial history, the Ghanaian international references tended to be European. What you saw of US culture was mostly in movies, especially gangster films. *The Godfather* was one of my favorites and my all-time favorite was *Scarface*, which I had watched multiple times in Moscow. It is another coincidence considering where my medical career took me, fixing facial deformities.

I arrived at the Lennons not as a refugee in search of a life but as someone moving on to the next step toward his destiny, and I was prepared. Knowing I would need my transcripts from Russia no matter where I was headed, every year I had them translated into English, officially stamped and verified, and mailed to London for safekeeping.

Suspicious Russian school officials asked me each time, "Why are you doing this?"

My answer, like the one I gave the visa clerk in Moscow, was true, but incomplete. "I'm on scholarship and I want to make sure that the people back at home, my family and the government, see that I'm doing well."

I mailed them all to a family friend in London so that when and if I could go the States, I wouldn't have to sneak those documents out, or have them discovered in my luggage and raise questions that could prevent me from leaving.

I also hedged my bets. I applied for a year's leave of absence from veterinary school. I never learned whether it was granted but I figured if all else failed, at least I wanted to finish that degree.

With all my worldly belongings and my modest nest egg, I bought my ticket to America. From London, I flew to Dallas, where I was to be hosted overnight and catch a connecting flight the following day. I stepped off the plane into the jetway and walked the final few steps out of my past with heightened awareness and a sense of foreboding. At the other end of that windowless tunnel I emerged into the bright bustling terminal with a spring in my step, a smile on my face, and my heart racing toward an uncertain future.

CHAPTER 7:
IF, IF, IF...

The word "if" now defined my life. Many if's needed to come true for me to somehow find a way to matriculate in a college or university so that I could try to get my visa amended to student status, which would allow me to stay and finish my education. I had made a commitment to myself to do it legitimately. I would not overstay my visa and be forced to live the life of a fugitive. I had made a decision that if nothing could be done by the day my visa was scheduled to expire, I would be getting on a plane and returning with great reluctance to Russia to complete my veterinary degree.

My choices were informed by the way my parents raised me—with an unwavering faith in God that a path had been designed for me and if I stayed on it, I would succeed in my goals. That path did not include breaking rules. If my visa expired, it meant the path was not supposed to be here in America—at least not now.

I was met in Dallas by a couple whose names I recognized as correspondents with my father, members of his loosely knit international missionary network. They knew quite a lot about my family and eagerly asked about my parents, particularly how my father's missionary work was going. It felt as though I had known them a long time instead of a few hours.

They were kind, thoughtful, and eager to explain everything I could see out the car windows. We drove from the airport to their home on a warm, humid Labor Day evening, September 7, 1992. The city was buzzing with sports fever—it was the first game of the football season for the Dallas Cowboys, who were hosting the Washington Redskins. I watched some of the game on television, fascinated by the bizarre-looking uniforms and the rugby-like intensity, none of it making any sense.

As wired up as I was, and although my biological clock was still on London time (six hours ahead), I slept fitfully that night and woke up eager to complete the final leg of my globe-girdling exodus from Russia. My host couple bid me farewell at the airport and I went to the ticket counter where it took some time to get the agent to understand my accent and my mangled pronunciation of Arkansas.

"I want to buy a ticket, one way, to Harrison Are…Kansas."

"Where?"

"Harrison, Are … KANsas."

When we had cleared that up, the agent asked me, "Are you sure? Harrison, Arkansas."

"Yes." With the language clumsiness they might have thought I was confused, or in the wrong airport, or had gotten the name of my destination mixed up.

She went to confer with one of her colleagues standing behind the counters. After some words were exchanged she returned with her supervisor. "Harrison, Arkansas," he said. "Sir, is that where you really want to go?"

"Yes!"

"Have you been there before?"

"No."

Why all these questions?

When I finally got my ticket and the plane began to board, I was surprised to see only a handful of people stand up, and shocked when I looked out the window at the smallest commercial aircraft I had even seen—a tail-dragger with one propeller. It had just a dozen or so seats crammed into a space so tiny you couldn't even halfway stand up. I was the only black person on board.

When the little plane descended for landing I could see no trace of a city or even a town. Just farmland and forest and a tiny airport. As soon as I was down the stairs and on the ground, I heard a familiar voice calling out my name—"DEREK!" Cindy ran out to the plane and threw her arms around me. I think she knew I might be rattled and wanted to wrap me in her love as fast as possible to make me feel safe. It worked.

She behaved as though she'd known me forever. After dropping my bags at the house, they drove me to her husband's workplace, a chain department store her husband managed. He proudly introduced me to everybody. The Lennons had apparently been so excited they had been telling everybody I was coming. It was a warm, open-hearted arrival.

There appeared to be not one other black person in Harrison, which explained why everyone seemed to wonder if

I was making a mistake. In the next several years that Harrison was my home away from home, I remember seeing only one other black person in a town of about 10,000, and that was a football player who had become a motivational speaker and came to give a talk to the high school football team. The family made a big fuss about making sure I met him.

In spite of what I found there, and in spite of what I learned later about the racial history of the area, I never felt especially out of place. I had lived in Russia, which was overwhelmingly white, so it wasn't a new thing to stick out, and from all reports Harrison was a much safer place than Moscow.

Soon after I arrived, my sister Elaine came to Harrison for a visit. It was such an uplifting experience to see one of my kind, especially one who I had a close connection with. Our anglicized names had been borrowed from an English singing duo, two children named Derek and Elaine who recorded inspirational music in the 1960s. We spent a few days together while I pondered my next step.

My visa was good for only six months. The Lennons fretted about the possibility I might have to return to Russia. IF I could, I wanted to stay—IF I could find a school that would have me, and IF I could find a way to pay my expenses. The Lennons said, "Let's see what we can do."

One day we went to visit another missionary family in Arkansas who lived across the street from the University of Central Arkansas in Conway, near the state capital of Little Rock.

I could almost hear something click in Cindy Lennon's mind when she said, "Hmm. There's a university. Derek, I think I want us to make a detour. Let's go to the international office for this school."

We found the office and Cindy ordered me to have a seat in the hall while she went in to investigate. After a long while she emerged with a man who reached out, shook my hand, and said, "Derek, I'm Brian Bolter. Welcome to the States. Cindy has been saying wonderful things about you. Are you interested in maybe having an education here?"

I had been a student in a medical school, so I assumed he meant resuming my medical studies. But then he asked, "Have you taken the SAT before?"

I had, when I was sixteen, more than five years earlier.

"What was your score?" I could only guess; it had been such a long time ago.

"Okay," he said. "Have you taken the Test of English as a Foreign Language (TOEFL)?"

I had and did remember my mark.

"Oh, that's a good score." Then Brian said in a matter-of-fact tone, "Well, I think we can get you a spot here."

I was stunned. Was it really so easy to get into medical school? Then it dawned on me that he was talking about earning an undergraduate degree first. I would have to repeat courses I had already taken.

Brian, Cindy and I sat down in his office and talked it through. I explained, "I really want to do human medicine, but I'm in veterinary medicine in Moscow and had gotten so far. I was hoping to apply to medical schools."

"Well, this is the way the US system works," Brian said. "You can't get into medical school directly. This is the only way you can do it." I was resigned to it, but thought no school would have me when they found out I had no money.

But Brian assured me, "We will find you some scholarship money. Don't worry about it. Go home, get these forms filled out, and send everything to me. I'll take it from there."

I got the forms filled out and mailed them back the next day. Two days later, Brian called to tell me that because the semester was already three weeks old, I would have to wait until the winter session, in January. That left me almost four months of waiting, and I did not have a student visa.

He said, "Don't worry about that. I'll take care of it for you."

From my research I knew that it was not so easy to get a visitor visa amended. The rule was that you had to go back to where you got the visa, meaning I would have to go back to Moscow, go to the US embassy, and hope I would be granted a new student visa. That, I was certain, was a very long and risky shot.

Brian seemed confident, so it looked as though I would be enrolled in school, with a scholarship and a student visa. It was a really good start, but I still needed to earn money to pay living and other expenses and I could not work without proper documentation. Fortunately, from my little business in Moscow selling clothing and imported shoes, and from working in London, I had saved enough money to carry me for a while.

Among the people I knew who were in the States was Daniel, a Ghanaian who had lived two houses away from where I grew up. He had come home on a visit when I was still in Accra and gave me his address. He had lived in Dallas a long time and had originally started out to become a veterinarian but never finished his schooling for lack of money. He had studied engineering instead.

He called as soon as he got my letter, and the first thing he said was, "You shouldn't be in Harrison. There's nothing for you there. I'll buy you a plane ticket; you come spend some time with me before school starts."

Daniel would prove to be a great friend and he helped me get a good start, but he made it clear up front, in the drive to his house from the airport, that I should not lean on him or expect too much. He said it many times, in many ways, like it was a lecture.

"I don't want you to think that you can rely on me the rest of your stay. You can't. You are on your own. In fact, don't rely on anybody. Whether you make it or you don't, it's up to you."

It seemed a strange way to break the ice when you've just picked somebody up from the airport, but later I realized he was making an assumption about me that wasn't true. Some Africans who come to the States to go to school are from wealthy families whose parents pay their tuition. Many of them flounder because they are not used to being on their own, typically live with relatives, and when they need something they just call home and get it. As a result, they fail to make good use of the opportunity.

I spent almost three months with Daniel, helping him in his high-end auto repair shop while I waited for my student visa to be approved. He was brilliant with cars and had quite a loyal following. I started out answering the phone and sweeping up. He was feeding me and giving me a place to live so I never expected any compensation. One day, after he had established that I was conscientious and dependable, he said he would give me a lump sum scholarship when it was time for me to go off to school. He wanted me to use it for something that would help me stay in school.

"Okay," I said. "I want you to teach me how to fix cars so that when I go to school I can fix cars for other students. I will use the money you give me to buy some tools and that's how I will earn my way through college."

He looked at me, shook his head, and laughed.

"You don't know anything about cars."

"Teach me."

I started with changing oil, and then fixing brakes, doing tune-ups, and so on. I worked hard to get it right and when I felt I had mastered the basics, I told Daniel, "I want a big job—a really big job."

There was a car that had been sitting in his garage that he had never touched, a Peugeot. "Whose car is that?"

"That belongs to a nurse. He wants to refurbish the engine but doesn't have the money."

"Why don't you show me what I need to do?"

A skeptical squint creased his face, but then he said, "Okay. If you can pull it off, I will let you have half the money when he pays for it."

I basically disassembled the engine and performed a major overhaul, replacing pistons and all the rest of the work that would put the motor in top condition. With Daniel's help, I got it all back together in perfect shape. The customer was overjoyed, found the money to pay for it, and I had $600.

I spent the money on some basic tools and a Volkswagen Rabbit so I could go back to Harrison from Conway on weekends and during semester breaks. When I wrote to my closest friend in Moscow, a fellow named Omega, he wrote back teasing me because I played the piano and, "You used to say pianists are always taking care of their fingers. Now you're getting your hands all greasy and oily? This is not you, is it?"

Daniel had quite an influence on me by giving me some wise advice based on his own experience. One day soon after I arrived he asked me what I really wanted to do.

"Medicine," I said. "But there's no way I can. I'm not going to find the money. I will have to study something else."

He told me more or less in passing that he regretted giving up on veterinary medicine. It had been his passion. What he said next I have never forgotten.

"Unless you plan on being dead in twenty years, twenty years is going to come, and it better find you doing the thing you really want to do. Don't give that dream up. Just keep at it. If that's what you really want to do, find a way to do it." It was exactly what I needed to hear.

Dan shared the story of his life in America, which was one of promise, struggle, and perseverance—not so different from mine and that of a lot of African immigrants. In the late 1970s he came to the US as a student to study veterinary medicine. While I had ended up in veterinary school against my desire, he loved horses and had been active in the horse racing world in Ghana.

His father had saved enough to underwrite his education but those careful plans were upended by the 1979 coup in Ghana. It caused a precipitous drop in the exchange rate for the Ghanaian currency, the cedi, and the new military government froze all foreign currency accounts. His family begged him to return home but he refused, recognizing that whatever opportunities he might have had there would be limited. The next five years were a struggle to survive, including periods of homelessness and starvation.

He mowed lawns, washed dishes, sold Bibles, and was blessed with the generosity of others. He gave up on veterinary medicine and enrolled at the University of Texas in Arlington to study mechanical engineering. His classmates never knew that he was at times homeless. A brilliant student, he could have landed a job at any of the big oil companies in Texas, had it been legally possible. He finally became an American citizen in 1986 and opened an automotive repair shop for high-end foreign cars.

In much the same way that barber shops serve as ad hoc community centers for African Americans, Dan's auto shop was more than a place to have your car fixed. It was a magnet for immigrants; a rendezvous on weekends to talk about everything from sports to life and African politics.

As a Johnny-come-lately, it was enlightening for me as well as entertaining to listen to the stories and arguments of some of these men who had been in the US for decades. There were former African politicians who seemed to always be on the defensive when the conversation touched on the failures of African governments.

Some were former athletes from Kenya and Ghana who at some point had represented their countries in the Commonwealth and Olympic games but now found themselves working menial jobs to make a living. There were those who came as students and had become executives in major corporations.

A Mr. Chang, originally from China, was a constant

presence at the auto shop. An executive with American Airlines, he stopped by the shop almost every night and on weekends, mostly to socialize and occasionally to have his car serviced. He shared with me his experiences as a student and some pearls of wisdom for successfully navigating the American educational system.

One of my former classmates from Prempeh boarding school heard I was in Dallas and came to visit me at the shop. After graduating from high school he emigrated to the States and ended up at Prairie View A&M University, a historically black university about an hour northwest of Houston, Texas. The school was popular among Africans because it was liberal with scholarships and in part because it claimed as a former student Laurence Tureaud, popularly known as the actor Mr. T, whose television character was known for the phrase, "I pity the fool." He also wore his hair in the style of a West African warrior of the Mandinka ethnic group.

My former schoolmate had been in America for six years, so I assumed he had completed his college degree and was working in a professional job. Instead, I learned he had quit school after two years, took a job in a factory earning $11 an hour, and drove a pricey car that was his pride and joy. He said he intended to go back to complete his college degree but three years after we had our little reunion, he had made no progress. I mention it because his experience is regrettably common among African immigrants who come to America intending to get a good education but have their heads turned by shiny new cars and easy money.

I returned from Dallas to Harrison for the Christmas

holiday in my Volkswagen Rabbit and Cindy helped me find and get set up in a shared apartment in Conway, where I would be attending school. But when I checked in with Brian Bolter, the man who had seemed so confident about being able to help me, I got the worst possible news—there was no scholarship after all.

"I don't have much money," I said. "All I have is the money that I brought. I can't go here without it. You told me that you were going to find — "

"Yes, I was going to," he said, "but it didn't pan out. Don't worry. We can probably figure something out where you can work and pay your tuition in bits." But first I needed my student visa and my visitor visa was set to expire on March 6, a date that was easy to remember because it is also Ghana's Independence Day.

The paperwork for the student visa had been filed with Brian Bolter's help, and he continued to reassure me that it was all going to work out. February came to an end with no mail from the US State Department. I eagerly checked the mailbox every day and every day felt my spirits sag a little further.

I began to contemplate the terrible possibility that in a few days I would have to chuck everything I had accomplished and use what money I had left to buy a ticket back to Moscow. It reminded me of waiting for the documentation I needed to go to medical school in Sweden, only to have it show up the day after I left for Russia. That had been a great disappointment. If it happened again, it would have been a crushing blow.

Monday, March 1, 1993, dawned. My stomach was all

knotted up. There was nothing in the mail but circulars. March 2, same thing. March 3 and March 4—nothing. I went to bed March 4 praying, "Please, God. If I don't get a visa tomorrow, I'm packing my stuff and I'm leaving."

I awoke March 5, a Friday, miserable, despondent, and feeling quite doomed. I had been going to the library every day to brush up on various subjects in preparation for my courses. I considered skipping the library that day but went anyway and then walked back to my lodgings with a hollow feeling in my gut and near tears. The sky was gray and a light spring drizzle fell.

I slowly opened the mailbox and there, crammed in, was a large envelope with a big, beautiful bald eagle on it and the words "US Immigration and Naturalization Service." My heart leaped. I carefully tore open the seal and there it was—a piece of paper that would determine the future path of my life.

In my wonderment I thought, Did they do it on purpose? Did they wait until the last day? But, why would they do that? I wanted to shout, but who could I shout this news to?

I slept soundly that night and awoke on Ghana Independence Day feeling like I had been holding my breath forever and could finally exhale. I was back on track towards my goal of becoming a doctor.

The school found me a job in the cafeteria and another in the library. Then the most amazing opportunity came along. The university language lab was having trouble finding someone to teach Russian. That paid a little bit better, so every week I would go to the bursar's office, endorse my paycheck over to the school, and they deducted it from my tuition bill. I had managed to dodge yet another bullet and had the satisfaction of knowing my Russian experience counted for something.

Back in classrooms again, it was odd being so much older than the other students, and many times more worldly by default. But lacking a social life had its advantages—I could focus exclusively on earning the best marks.

CHAPTER 8: AFRICANS EVERYWHERE!

A well-known inspirational story in the global community of Christian missionaries and their supporters is a modern version of the Biblical loaves-and-fishes miracle that Jesus is recorded to have performed to feed thousands of hungry followers. The modern story is about a Prussian, George Müller, who emigrated to England in 1829, became a preacher, and went on to build and manage orphanages that educated thousands of homeless and abandoned children.

The story may be somewhat apocryphal but, according to the accounts passed down over the years, the kitchen ran out of food so that one morning there was nothing to feed the children for breakfast. Müller is said to have ordered the housemother to seat the children in the dining room as usual and he led them in a prayer for help. Within minutes there was a knock on the front door. The town baker had a vision or dream the night before that prompted him to bake extra bread for the orphanage.

Then the driver of a milk cart showed up. His axle had broken and it would take so long to fix that the milk would spoil before it could be delivered. He wanted to know if the orphanage could use it.

I'm convinced the story is true because it happened once to my family. It was a low point when we sat down to an empty table because we'd had no money to buy food. Instead, my father led us in prayer, blessing food that wasn't there. As we were praying there was a knock on the door. Some kind people in the neighborhood had prepared us a meal and brought it to us ready to eat. Had I not witnessed it, I wouldn't believe it.

There have been many George Müller experiences in my life but there is one that was especially inspirational and it happened in a most unlikely place, on a bitter cold night in a remote, seemingly inhospitable part of northern Arkansas. I was driving the VW Rabbit that I'd bought in Dallas, returning to the Lennons from school for the Christmas break. With me were two fellow students, women from Guinea, a former French colony on Africa's west coast, north of Ghana.

I had stayed true to my commitment about not dating until I was married. These students were part of a social circle at school of young Africans who had found each other largely by sight. Many Africans will tell you that they can spot another African across a room full of black Americans. We are typically darker than black Americans, our heads and faces have distinctive shapes, and we dress a bit more as we would at home than in the prevailing styles here.

Just as the veterinary students did in Moscow, African students at the University of Central Arkansas tended to gravitate toward those who shared a common continental heritage, uniquely shaped by tribalism and colonialism. These two Guinean women were among the first Africans I met and I was excited for them to meet the Lennons and share an American Christmas with them.

The road from Conway to Harrison is about a hundred miles, all but a few of them through sparsely settled farm and timber country. At night it was an endless, dark, winding drive. You could travel long stretches without seeing another car. There are just three very small towns along the route and my car coughed and died just outside one of them, Marshall. It is the seat of a county so rural the town's population then was only about 1,300, all but a handful of whom were white.

Marshall is in a remote, backwoods-y pocket of the country that, during the early 1900s, had been ethnically cleansed of African Americans by anti-black race riots, lynchings, and the destruction or seizure of black-owned properties. In Harrison, anti-black harassment and violence between 1905 and 1909 drove all but one of its black residents out of town and out of that part of the state.

That area of the Ozark Mountains became a sanctuary for a faction of the Ku Klux Klan, a secret organization of white supremacists whose signature terror tactic was the burning of crosses in front of black homes and churches. Arkansas's capital, Little Rock, later became a flash point in the civil rights movement, one that historians consider the most severe test of the US Constitution since the Civil War. Ironically, the little town of Marshall was named after the fourth

Chief Justice of the US Supreme Court, John Marshall, who played a major role in the evolution of the American legal system that would make the civil rights movement possible.

Some of this history I had heard about and some I learned later. I knew that racial animosity was considered a problem because Cindy had warned me to fill my gas tank before leaving Conway, to drive at night, and to not stop for any reason until I got to the Lennons' house in Harrison.

I mention this history, and the sense of danger at the time, not to denigrate any people or communities, nor am I ignoring that things have gotten better in the past two decades. I bring it up because African American history meant something to me personally. I had grown up keenly aware that the region I come from was a slave-trading center and embarkation point to the Americas.

Although I put my faith in God and His plan for me, like most Africans I had learned the challenges of social acceptance and personal safety. I had studied and seen the effects of tribal and colonial persecution in Africa, I had seen and heard about the treatment of Africans in Moscow, and now I was learning about the treatment of black people in parts of America.

So when my car sputtered and rolled to a stop on the shoulder on that dark, lonely highway, I was afraid. A quick check under the hood confirmed the problem was beyond fixing myself, so I had to find a telephone to call the Lennons for help. In the distance, across a field, a light shone. It looked like a house.

"I have to go find a telephone to get help," I told the women. "Do not get out of the car, lock the doors, and do not talk to anyone who might come along." I felt bad leaving them there but it seemed safer than the three of us traipsing around in the dark.

I hiked across the field, stumbling on the frozen, uneven earth until I found myself in an auto junkyard with a trailer home in the middle. I knocked on the front door and waited, worrying, hoping, praying that everything would turn out all right.

The door opened a crack and a young man, unshaven with long hair, wearing a T-shirt and holding a can of beer, peered out.

"What the … !"

"I'm so sorry to disturb you, but my car just broke down on the road and I need to contact someone to come get me and my friends. I wonder, if you have a phone could I make a call?"

He looked over my head. "Where at's your friends?"

"They are in the car. Can you help me, please?"

He hesitated a moment. A television was on in the background—a Western gun fight. He shrugged and pushed the door wide enough for me to enter. "Sure. C'mon in. I ain't got a phone but I can give you a ride into town. They got a phone booth there. Hey, baby!" he called out. "C'mere a minute."

A young woman in a sweatshirt and sweatpants came out from a room in the back. I explained my predicament.

"It's awful cold," she said. "Why don't you get those girls and bring 'em in here? I'll make some tea while you all go make your phone call."

With great trepidation, I led the Guineans to the house,

left them with the young woman, climbed into the passenger seat of a tow truck, and rode into Marshall with the young man. He spun the steering wheel with a knob handle as he pulled out onto the highway. In the glow of the dash his hands looked rough for his age, with knuckles chapped like a mechanic's. I recognized them from my days helping Daniel in his business.

"Ya know," he said, "I just got outta jail three days ago."

My heart began to thump.

"I done somethin' real bad. Don't matter what it was, but I was a couple years down to Cummins. It's a real bad prison, I'll tell you what. Even made a movie 'bout it, with Robert Redford. Maybe you seen it. Well, I been in a few prisons, to be truthful. But this time, I figgered when I got out I'm really gonna try and turn my life around."

He picked up a pack of cigarettes on the dash, shook one out and offered it to me.

"No, thank you."

He lit one, the match flame throwing shadows that outlined a scar on his stubbled cheek.

"Well, when I opened the door and there you was, come right outta nowhere, first thing I says to myself, I says, Somebody up there is tellin' me to be a Good Samaritan and help you out. So here I am. Where was it you all came from, anyway? You must of got lost pretty bad to end up in this godforsaken podunk town."

When I got Cindy on the phone and explained my plight, she sounded even more alarmed than I had been earlier. "Oh, Lord, Derek! You're stuck in Marshall! Are you all right? Where are you? Where are your friends?"

I handed the phone to the young man, my Samaritan, so he could explain to Cindy where he lived. "Yes, ma'am, that's the one, the junkyard just south of Marshall on 65 ... Yes, ma'am. I'll take good care of 'em. ... Don't you worry none 'bout that. ... God bless you too, ma'am."

Cindy knew exactly where the house was because she'd driven that road so many times and remembered there was a handmade sign out front of the junkyard, a memorial of sorts for a child who had been killed by a drunk driver. It took her an hour to reach us. The young man, whose name I regrettably never recorded, towed my car off the road into his junkyard and made a pass at trying to fix it while the young woman made more tea for us and put out some snacks. Between all our accents—mine Ghanaian, the women with their Guinean French, our host with her American Southern—there was a lot of repeating, but somehow we managed to make ourselves understood.

When Cindy arrived and we were about to leave, I thanked the man and insisted he take some money, which he did after not much cajoling. As poor as I was, he was clearly poorer.

"Derek, man, I ain't never gonna forget you all. God sent you to give me a message. I'm sure of it. And I got the message, loud 'n clear. I'm gonna turn my life around. I really am. God bless you, man. You come and see us sometime, any time."

I have often wondered over the years how he made out, and wished I could thank him again.

"You are one blessed young man, Derek," Cindy said on the drive through the dark hills to Harrison. "If you had been on the other side of Marshall, there's no telling what would have happened. I don't know that anybody would have taken you in."

I did feel blessed, in many ways. While I missed my family that Christmas—my fourth far from home—my African friends, including others from school that Cindy had extended an invitation to, managed to approximate the experience of an extended African family. The Lennon home filled up with students made temporarily homeless by the winter break, including my sister Elaine. People were sleeping wherever they could find room, on sofas and floors. Cindy came down early one morning to start cooking breakfast, looked around, and declared, "Good Lord, there are Africans everywhere!"

The Lennons worked hard to make it a fun Christmas, helping to take the sting out of everyone's homesickness. By their smiles, laughter, and generosity of spirit the Lennons showed they were having the most exotic, fun time of their lives. It wasn't hard for me to imagine that my home would have been just as exciting and fun if a gang of American college students showed up for Christmas. As it was, when I was younger and when we had the space, our home was often overflowing with extended family and travelers. The chaos was somehow comforting.

Christmas in Ghana is just as big a deal as it is in America, although the traditions I grew up with were modest. For many families, Christmas was when children got their new clothes for the coming year. It was such a thrill the first time my mother took me to the tailor to be measured for new pants and shirts and a jacket. We called those outfits political suits because that's what politicians wore.

You could always tell which children had been to the tailor because they would proudly wear their new outfits to church on Christmas morning. It was common to see siblings show up in the same colors and fabrics because their mothers had gotten a good price on a bolt. The lucky child might also get an accessory or two—a toy watch or spectacles or a funny party hat. Large heels on men's shoes—platform shoes— were in fashion in those days. They were called guarantees, I suppose because the heels were so big they never wore out. Afros were popular, as were shirts with enormous collars. Whatever James Brown and other American cultural icons wore, we wanted to wear.

On Christmas Day, houses and villages filled with the aroma of boiling chicken, turkey, or goat meat, pepper soup, and the thumping of the pestle and mortar for fufu. The best part of Christmas for all children was the building of a Christmas house. The kids in each neighborhood, and in each village in rural areas, would get together, organize themselves, and then go out to cut and gather palm fronds and sticks. When all the raw materials had been assembled, we'd work together lashing up a stick frame with strips of bark and then weaving and lashing the palm fronds onto it. When it was done it was a little hut that we used as a neigh-borhood playhouse.

When the groups of children finished their Christmas houses, they would walk around the other neighborhoods or villages to see who had the best one, the one where everyone else wanted to hang out. If yours wasn't the most popular, you and your friends would start planning how to make it bigger and fancier next year.

In the quiet moments by myself, or as I fell asleep, these memories brought a lump to my throat and fueled my resolve to succeed in becoming a doctor, a goal that I could not have achieved without a few more George Müller miracles.

CHAPTER 9:
AMONG THE
SAMARITANS

Because I would be working off my tuition while earning the credits I needed for medical school as opposed to paying it in advance as other students had, I was unable to register for classes ahead of time. When I showed up that first semester, the registrar told me the only classes left open were senior-level courses that had prerequisite studies I had completed years earlier and filed away in the deep recesses of my memory.

Yes, I had studied calculus, but in two years of veterinary school it hadn't been useful. I knew I was going to have a hard time and my visa status left no wiggle room if I failed. My fear became real the first day when my chemistry professor announced that we would all have to take a pre-calculus test, "to see where everybody is." My stomach was in knots as I handed in mine. I knew it was a disaster.

When the professor passed out our graded tests a few days later, he warned, "Some of you are not going to last two weeks in here, so you might want to start thinking about a Plan B."

I stared at my flunking grade with a sinking heart and a hot wave of shame. Throughout veterinary school, I had made all A's. I had no Plan B. I had, however, met more than my share of obstacles by that time so my thinking, faithful self came to the rescue—I was just not going to be one of those who didn't last.

In between classroom time and working my tuition-paying jobs, I buried myself in my books, trying to recall work I had done with skills I had not used for five years. Two weeks or so later we sat for the first exam of the course. I knew I had done well but I enjoyed the warm glow of pride when I got it back with a perfect score—one hundred.

It didn't take long for word to get around that this black guy—Okay, he's from Africa, but he's a black guy!—had just waltzed in out of nowhere and pulled off a perfect exam in a 400-level class. How was that possible?

As unusual a classmate as I must have seemed for all those reasons, the one that might have left the strongest impression was my use of a common lab tool called a pipette. A pipette is a slender, calibrated glass tube that you use to draw up a volume of fluid so that it can be measured out in precise milliliters for experiments and tests.

Most of the pipettes in that lab were unrecognizable to me. They had mechanical controls that created the suction to draw up the solution. I had no idea how to use them. The only pipettes I had ever seen were in Ghana—the kind you might have found in an American high school chemistry lab in the 1960s. You dip the tip of the tube in the solution, put your mouth over the open end, and draw like you do a drinking straw, only gently and carefully to avoid ingesting the fluids.

When you have drawn up enough liquid you quickly put your thumb over the open end to create a vacuum so nothing will drain out. Then, by releasing your thumb a little, you allow the fluid to escape slowly from the narrow tip and, using the calibration marks on the tube as a guide, add the desired quantity to the test tube or other vessel you're working with.

Pipetting by mouth without much experience can lead to accidentally ingesting a corrosive substance or, in a medical lab, an infectious bacteria. By some estimates, the use of oral pipetting in medical laboratories used to be the cause of one out of five lab worker infections. By the 1980s, mouth pipetting had essentially been eradicated in the US. It was the only way I had ever done it and I was experienced, so I just took one of the old-fashioned pipettes that was there and began to draw up some acetone, a highly toxic solvent.

As I worked I could almost feel the professor staring at me and when I checked he was indeed standing with his arms folded, gazing with eyes narrowed and brow knitted. Then he picked up a mechanical pipette from another table and strode over to my station.

He held it out. "You know, you can use this instrument. See?" He demonstrated. "It does the job and less chance of an accident."

"Oh, okay." It made no difference to me, but the way the

rest of the students were stealing glances in my direction and stifling titters made me a little self-conscious. Knowing what I do now, it's a funny story. I imagine the professor must have enjoyed a chuckle with his colleagues later about the kid from Ghana.

"Can you believe it? They still pipette by mouth over there! They probably still use rocks to wash their clothes, too."

By the time we'd taken the second exam, after I scored another perfect mark, I had mastered the mechanical pipettes and I was a popular lab and study partner.

It was in the chemistry department that I met my next Samaritan. Everyone who helped me along my path is dear to me, but this person holds a special place for having taken a couple of leaps of faith that finally made it possible for me to go to medical school. His name was Professor Jerald "Jerry" M. Manion. Dr. Manion was the former chairman of the chemistry department and the faculty advisor for pre-med students at the University of Central Arkansas. He taught a course in organic spectroscopy, the study of the molecular structure of organic molecules.

When I first met with him as my pre-med advisor, he explained that the odds were stacked against me.

"You should know, Derek, that it's rare for an international student to get into medical school in the United States." His confident, businesslike explanation made it clear this was a familiar conversation.

"Many of the state-supported schools, including our College of Medicine at the University of Arkansas, were founded by physicians to prepare other physicians to practice in their own state. Ours was started by eight Little Rock doctors in 1879. So, not only do they not take students from Ghana, but they rarely take American students from other states. When they do, the out-of-state students have to meet much higher standards and the tuition is doubled. An international student like you is going to be limited to private medical schools."

When I had been a Ghanaian boy, I had dreamed of going to medical school. When the first school that accepted me, the University of Rochester, required me to pay the entire $160,000 tuition in advance, I was disappointed but I didn't give up. In the end I sent out a hundred or more applications to medical schools all over the globe.

Now a Ghanaian man, and in spite of the physical danger, I was prepared to return to Moscow to finish the veterinary degree I hadn't sought and didn't intend to use, if that were to be my only choice. In the meantime, Dr. Manion's splash of reality was helpful but I was more convinced than ever that God's plan was for me to become a physician and use my skills to bring better healthcare to Ghana. How that would happen remained unknown but not, I was convinced, impossible.

Among the knowns was the fact that I needed to take Dr. Manion's spectroscopy course in order to graduate. I wanted to complete my pre-med requirements as quickly as possible, but his course was being offered at the same time as another class I needed to graduate. Waiting another year to take mass spectroscopy meant waiting another year to graduate which, in turn, would have required me to take and pay for the minimum number of credits to maintain my status as an international student.

With nothing to lose, I went to see him one day to plead my case. "I was wondering if it would be possible to register but not attend class and allow me to take the test at the end and, if I pass, give me credit toward my graduation requirements."

He agreed, but instead of letting me skip classes he arranged to give me private lessons outside class and allowed me to take the test at the end. I got my passing grade and my credit. That was the sum total of our interaction—tutor/advisor and student. He was accommodating and kind, but it was a professional relationship, which made what happened later all the more surprising.

Unlike Harrison, Conway had a black community and it had a small but tightly knit network of international students and foreign-born residents. One of my biology professors came to me one day and said, "There's a family here in Conway, very well known, who you may be related to. Your names sound the same."

I recognized the name. "I know they're from Ghana, but it's not quite the same name. So we aren't related."

"Well, is it okay if I give them your information anyway? They're very good people."

The couple, James and Lydia, ended up becoming good family friends. Like myself, James came to the US as a student. He was later joined by his wife and children. James worked as medical technologist and Lydia was a teacher and social worker.

They were a kind family. There were times I would go back to my apartment from class and find a basket of food at the door with an encouraging card. They had a two-year-old son who thought of me as his big brother and still does.

Whenever I saw James he would ask me how school was going and whether I had taken the Medical College Admission Test (MCAT) yet. The MCAT is a standardized exam that is a major factor in deciding whether a medical school will admit a student. I kept putting it off because the fee was expensive, about $200 or so.

Every time we met he would ask, "Have you taken the MCAT?"

Every time I would say, "Oh, next month, probably."

A month would pass and he'd ask me again, and again I'd say, "Next month." I didn't want to tell him the reason because I wanted to avoid causing him to feel obligated to help or seem as though I was trying to solicit it.

Finally, one day he came to see me and handed me a large envelope. Inside were all the forms needed to register to take the MCAT, forms you could only get by paying the fee. He had done it on his own.

"Okay, Derek. No more excuses. Now, fill it out."

I was speechless with emotion. All I could do was shake my head. I was truly living among Samaritans.

With the MCAT behind me, and a good score, I began the process of applying to medical schools. In spite of Dr. Manion's warning, I included the University of Arkansas College of Medicine (UAMS), fully expecting to be turned down. Among the others was Meharry Medical College in Nashville, Tennessee. Meharry had been founded in 1876 to educate black doctors who could serve the populations of freed slaves that most white physicians refused to treat and most Southern hospitals refused to admit.

UAMS was in Little Rock and would be more convenient to the Lennons, although my tuition would be about $12,000 for each year of the four-year program, twice that of in-state students. Nevertheless, I was thrilled and feeling just a bit smug when I was granted early admission in January 1994. I would start that August.

Meharry also was interested and although I had already been accepted at Arkansas, I drove to Nashville for the interview. On the way I was afraid I'd be late and was stopped by a policeman for speeding. He was intrigued by my last name—he could not pronounce it and asked where I was going.

"I'm going to Nashville, for a medical school interview."

"Okay, Mr. Bo Heeny. Good luck but please drive carefully. We need more good doctors."

My interest in Meharry was not so keen since I had a slot at Arkansas. I couldn't ignore the fact that Meharry was known to be struggling financially and that a few years earlier a National Science Foundation study of the best and worst US medical schools ranked it last. A National Medical Association study around the same time found that Meharry graduates had lower rates of board certification than graduates of other medical schools. In the end, I wasn't offered a spot that year, which seemed to confirm that I was all set.

The early admission by Arkansas gave me eight months to earn the tuition I'd need for the first year. The US Immigration Service granted my application for a work visa and my biology professor, Dr. Moran, offered me a position as a research assistant in his physiology research lab. He was studying the function of chloride channels in the intestine of a sea creature called the California sea hare, a large variety of slug. This research was important in understanding the function of chloride channels, which, when malfunctional, cause cystic fibrosis, a genetic disease that affects and kills many children around the world. Dr. Moran became an important and valued mentor through my stay in college and later when I was in graduate school.

That extraordinary opportunity almost didn't happen because of a landlady who had a grudge against Africans. I had rented a room in a four-bedroom house about two miles from the school campus. The owner was a middle-aged recently widowed woman who lived with her son and daughter, both about my age.

In addition to the rent, out of respect, I offered to pitch in with the household chores. It quickly became apparent, and quite depressing, that the landlady now considered me her servant. Initially I helped with the dishes, cleaning, gardening, and other chores that her children refused to do.

She began demanding more and more of my time and took to ordering me about, until I finally had enough and explained that I was trying to be helpful but I was not her servant. She flew into a rage and began lecturing me about "you lazy, rich Africans." There was no reasoning with her.

Frustrated, I went to the pastor at my church to explain what was going on and to ask him to help me find a place for the last two weeks of the semester. He said that instead of running away from the problem I should take the opportunity to show her Christian principles. I had no spare time for such a project so I just ran out the clock for those final weeks by leaving the house as soon as I awoke and returning late, just to sleep.

When Dr. Moran called her house looking for me to tell

me about the research assistantship, the woman warned him not to offer me the position. "He's just one of those lazy rich Africans who don't need the money or the experience." Happily, he ignored her advice.

That summer, I also got a job as a lab assistant for a nursing class. Each week it was my job to fetch fresh cow hearts and livers from the local slaughterhouse and prepare them for dissection. My experience dissecting cows and horses came in handy. Finally I was doing something relevant to human medicine, and I was going to be enrolled in medical school! I wrote home with the good news.

CHAPTER 10:
DON'T LET ME DOWN

My father—otherwise know to his parishioners as Evangelist James—was invited to visit the US in 1995 to speak about his missionary work at various churches and retreats. His travel plans coincided with my summer break from school, allowing us to be reunited for the first time in nearly five years, ever since the day I waved goodbye as I boarded a Moscow-bound jet in Accra.

He came to Conway and it was my turn to welcome a Ghanaian to Harrison's tiny airport. It was one of the happiest days of my life, seeing him and having so much to tell about my experiences and so many questions to ask about my mother, siblings, and other relatives back home.

He spoke at a summer camp retreat nearby, so for the first time I got to hear what he had been telling people about his life, our family, and God's clear intervention in our lives. He talked about how he became a Christian and about his missionary work in Ghana's villages. It is one thing to be a member of a family with such a history, but another to sit in an audience of close to six hundred people who were listening intently as my father shared it from a podium, seeing how moved and inspired everyone seemed to be. I was fiercely proud of him.

He had speaking engagements in several states so instead of flying he insisted on driving with me. One of the trips took us to Indiana, a long trek that became an unforgettable father-son bonding experience. It was so much fun telling him about the crazy time in Russia, now that it was far behind me.

Just before we left on that trip I got my grades for the previous semester in the mail. With a hint of mischief in my voice, I said, "Father, I have gotten my report card. Are you interested in seeing my grades?"

He laughed. Bringing home report cards was a major ritual when I was growing up. It was always the first thing he asked about when he returned home from a business trip.

This time, I told him he could only see my grades if he promised to pay my tuition for the next semester. It was just a joke and he knew it. There was no way he could afford it. But I regretted the remark as I studied his face when he looked at my grades, straight A's. His lower lip quivered and his eyes shimmered with unshed tears.

"This is very impressive, my son. You know I will do anything to support you. I would pay your tuition if I could, but all I can do for you now is pray."

Now it was my turn to shed a tear. "Father, your prayers are being answered."

It had been a point of pride as well as practicality that I never had to impose on my parents for money. Whether I was selling jeans in Moscow or fixing cars in Dallas, I always watched my pennies, so much so that I became notorious among my friends. I ate a lot of rice because it was cheap to buy in ten-pound sacks. I seasoned it with individual-portion packets of ketchup that were left over from fast food restaurants and ate scrambled eggs for protein. It didn't seem quite so bad to me at the time. Having lived through a famine in 1983, witnessing the suffering of refugees from Chad when I was growing up in Ghana, and being aware of the suffering of millions of others on the continent, my situation hardly seemed dire.

The job I had gotten at a furniture factory in Conway was on an assembly line putting together school furniture. It was hard work, the sort of job that would have motivated most people to pursue school. Among other tasks, we assembled boxes with scalding hot glue. People frequently suffered painful burns.

As I have often done, I told my coworkers stories about my life and tried to encourage them to aspire to be more. "You can't do this your whole life. You could take some night classes. Keep at it and you'll make it." How odd it must have seemed to them, living in the land of opportunity and being lectured to strive for more by a poor boy from Ghana.

One morning I rushed off to work in such a hurry that during the lunch break I had a sudden misgiving that I had left the tea kettle on the stove with the burner lit. I lived just five minutes away so during the lunch break I drove back to the apartment, relieved to discover that I had turned it off.

When I returned a few minutes later the guard at the

security gate refused to admit me. "You're not allowed to leave the premises during lunch."

"I didn't know," I explained. "I just ran home long enough to make sure I didn't leave my stove on."

The guard picked up a phone in his shack and spoke to someone. When he hung up he said, "Okay, you can come in. But tomorrow morning you have to check in with the main office."

I did and was told, "You're fired."

I was close to starting medical school, so it didn't matter from a practical standpoint. But I did not like the idea of being fired so I went back and tried to reason with the boss.

"Would you rather see the firefighters hosing down a house with everything in it burned or a safety-conscious employee?" I argued. "I didn't know there was a policy against leaving during work breaks. Nobody told me. And I used my lunch break, not company time."

My plea carried the day. I was reinstated and my name was cleared. I worked one more week and then quit.

A short while later I saw an ad for a job in Conway with a startup software company that paid almost twice what I had been earning at the furniture factory. It was a data-entry position that required being able to type at least thirty words per minute without making any mistakes. I didn't know how to type so I spent hours practicing until I thought I could do it.

But when I went in to apply and take the test, I couldn't quite hit the mark. I tried multiple times but kept coming up a word or two short. The woman who was giving the test told me, "Everything you've done here looks good, but you just aren't quite fast enough. Why don't you take a couple days and practice, then come back and try again."

I did and failed again, by one word. She let me come back a third day but I still couldn't break through. By this time, having encouraged me to keep coming back, she and I had formed a temporary bond. I was so close to passing but she said unless I could hit the thirty words, she couldn't hire me.

"Really?" I said. "Do you think that one word would make a difference?"

"No, not really. But that's the requirement."

It was such a minor thing but I was competitive and unaccustomed to failing. My spirit sagged and I sighed heavily. As I gathered my belongings to leave she said, "So, how's your dad?"

That was a jolt. "My dad? Uh, my dad is fine, but I don't think you know him."

"Oh, yeah," she said, smiling. "I know your dad. In fact, I know about your family, too."

"But ... how?"

"Well, a few months back I went to a summer Bible camp and a guy came to talk to us, from Africa. He mentioned that he has a son who goes to school here and considering there aren't many Africans from Africa around here, it must be you."

She had attended the retreat that my father had spoken at. I was delighted to know that someone had been touched by my father's work and was reminded to always conduct myself honorably and graciously, no matter how obscure or inconsequential the circumstances may seem. God was always watching, and some of his flock were as well.

August finally rolled around and about a week before school was to begin I drove to the college, full of hope and anticipation, to complete some admissions paperwork. But the clerk who was serving me returned from a search for my records to tell me I would have to speak with the admissions officer. Of course, there was a problem.

"We didn't realize that you were a foreign student," I was told. "You aren't eligible to do your studies here."

It was just as Dr. Manion had warned, yet it made no sense.

"This is news," I said, my heart pounding. "My admissions paperwork clearly states that I am an out-of-state international student and my tuition will be double the fee for everybody else. I have the letter stating all this. I hid nothing and the college acknowledged my status in accepting me. And I am prepared to pay the tuition."

"I'm sorry but we can't enroll you here. This is a state university. There's nothing we can do."

It was a repeat of what had happened in Ghana when I had won a scholarship to study in Germany only to have it taken away without warning or explanation. This turnabout left me stunned but also suspicious. There was something fishy going on and Dr. Manion agreed. "This is not going to happen to you, Derek. We won't let this happen to you." The roller coaster of my life was beginning to feel endless.

Some people advised me to sue the school. I didn't even understand what that entailed at first, but when it was explained I couldn't see how it would help. If I succeeded in forcing them to take me, it would have been an awkward situation. I would probably have been subjected to close scrutiny and even distrust.

In the end I won a pyrrhic sort of compromise. I agreed

to sign a statement saying I would defer my admission voluntarily until I became a resident of the state. "We'll see what happens next year," Dr. Manion said. "We'll try and see if the state government can help."

It was not much of a compromise, I knew, because to become a resident meant getting a green card and that wasn't going to happen any time soon. Once again, the goal was so close yet so far away.

Now I had a new problem—how to finesse my visa status. As a foreign student I could not be out of school even for a semester. Unless I could show I was enrolled I would have to return to Russia. The solution was to enroll at University of Central Arkansas as a graduate student studying physiology. Because I was again late to the party, so to speak, all the graduate scholarships had been given away. I had to pay my way, but I had saved enough to cover the cost.

With a heavy heart, I began again the process of applying to medical schools, but this time I applied only to private schools. While I was doing that, I received an unsolicited invitation from Meharry to return for another interview.

Although Meharry had not been my first choice the first time around, the school was in the process of obtaining more reliable funding, working to improve its reputation, and getting some positive recognition. A Meharry graduate, Dr. Audrey Forbes Manley, had just been appointed acting Surgeon General of the United States, in January 1995.

Meharry graduates were starting to win prestigious residency spots. One student had just gone on to do his internship at the Mayo Clinic. Meharry was not a state school that might change its mind at the last minute, and they seemed eager to have me. I accepted their offer, praying that this time I would have better luck.

The following year, I received an admission letter from UAMS offering me a spot in the class beginning in 1995. I politely deferred the admission and joined the class at Meharry. I have kept all those letters as a reminder and motivation to my siblings who were to follow my footsteps years later into medical school.

As institutions go, Meharry has one of the most interesting histories, having witnessed and survived nearly 140 turbulent years in American racial history. What makes it particularly interesting and relevant to me is the story of its founder, Samuel Meharry, who had a profound experience much like mine on that cold dark night when my car broke down in a remote corner of the Ozarks.

Meharry was sixteen years old and his vehicle was a wagon loaded with sacks of salt. It was in the 1820s in the relative wilds of Kentucky. It was raining and dusk was gathering when the wagon he was driving slid off the muddy road into a ditch and got stuck. As I had, Meharry set out on foot to look for help.

The story goes that he found a modest cabin in the woods, occupied by a slave family that had escaped their bondage and had bounties on their heads, reward money that a slave hunter could collect if they were caught and returned to their masters. Risking their freedom by trusting that Meharry, who was white, would not turn them in, they fed and sheltered him for the night. In the morning they helped get him and his wagon back on the road and on his way.

Meharry was so grateful that he promised the family that

if he ever made any money he would do something "for your race." Forty or so years later, he and his three brothers put up $30,000 in cash and real estate to start a medical college for former slaves. At Meharry today, the Salt Wagon story is still told and there is a cafe in the school called the Salt Wagon.

Of course, as usual, there was a problem. As an international student I wasn't eligible for government-backed loans to pay for my tuition, which at a private school was not subsidized by state funding and thus much higher. A lady from church, a nurse, agreed to be cosigner on a loan but her income wasn't enough to satisfy the bank. I needed another cosigner and had run out of options. Once again, so close yet so far away. I prayed and tried to keep up my faith that somehow things would work out.

As August approached, my hopes began to fade and as the days left to me to register dwindled, I realized that I had to accept that God's plan did not include going to medical school, at least not now. I dreaded the possibility that I might have to return to Russia, or go home to Ghana with my dream unfulfilled.

One day I was walking through the campus at Central Arkansas when some joggers came running past. One of them stopped and turned.

"Derek!" It was Dr. Manion. "How have you been? You must be getting ready to go off to Nashville. You're finally on your way."

I looked away for a moment, to hide my feelings.

"Dr. Manion, I ... I can't go after all. There's a problem."

"A problem? At this late date? What is it?"

"I need a qualified cosigner for my loans."

He fixed me with a steady gaze for a few moments.

"Maybe I can help. Do you have the application papers?"

"In my apartment."

"Go get them, then. Meet me back here, in front of the science building."

I ran the entire way and back. Gasping for breath I handed him the forms.

"You understand I have to discuss this with my wife first. Why don't you come see me in my office tomorrow and I'll let you know."

My hopes had soared but when he mentioned his wife, they sank again and I suffered through another restless night, praying but trying to tamp down my expectations. She would be practical, I told myself, and point out to him what a risky thing it was to cosign a loan for a foreign student he barely knew.

I entered his office the next morning with my heart in my throat.

He looked and smiled broadly. "Derek! Come in, have a seat. This shouldn't take long."

He retrieved the loan application from a stack of papers, silently looked it over for a moment, and then pulled out his pen and began to write, flipping the pages one by one and scribbling on each. My eyes stung with tears of silent gratitude.

Finally, he put his pen down and handed me the papers.

"Okay, Derek, that should do it. I'm your other cosigner now. I'm sure you won't have a problem getting the bank to accept it. I've never done anything like this before, but it just isn't fair what happened with Arkansas and I have a feeling you're going to do well. All I ask is that you don't let me down."

CHAPTER 11:
FROM CARCASSES
TO CADAVERS

No one could have been happier than I was to have found a way around the last obstacle between me and my medical training. James, the Ghanaian man in Conway who had paid for my MCAT exam, came as close as anyone. He insisted on helping me move my belongings to Nashville, where I had arranged to rent an apartment I'd found advertised in a newspaper. I didn't have time to go see it so I made all the arrangements by phone.

"This apartment is very nice," the rental agent had said. "It's next to a golf course, not too far from the Meharry campus. We have some Meharry students who live here."

When we found the address, both James and I were horrified. It was a rundown housing project. Yes, there was a golf course nearby, but it was separated from the apartments by a ditch full of trash and discarded furniture. I didn't like the look of the residents, who reminded me of people I had seen in movies depicting inner-city squalor and drug-dealing.

I come from a country that has more than its share of poverty, but nothing I had seen at home could compare with the sense of danger and despair I felt. No one had to tell me it was a crime-ridden neighborhood, but statistically Nashville's crime rate at the time was one of the worst in the nation.

As James eased his pickup truck into a parking spot, I said, "This is not a place I would be found in morning, afternoon, night—never." He just nodded.

I decided to put my things in the apartment since James had to return to Conway. In the morning I would look for a place that felt safer. But when I opened the door the stench of rotting food that had been left in the refrigerator was overwhelming. When I turned on the light in the kitchen swarms of cockroaches scattered into the crevices behind the baseboards and backsplashes.

With the greatest reluctance, we unloaded the truck. Fortunately, the apartment had a small balcony where we stacked everything and closed the sliding glass door. I hoped the cockroaches would be less likely to infest anything before I could find another place to live, and that no scoundrel would notice and rob me before I could move it all.

By the time I got to the rental office to speak to the manager, I was in a rare state of outrage. "You lied to me and took my deposit." Of course, there was nothing he would do about it. It was a dispiriting start.

I knew no one in Nashville and hadn't even checked in with Meharry yet. I telephoned a childhood friend from

Ghana named Ben who was living in Conway and vented my frustration. His parents were native Ghanaians who had emigrated to the States where he was born and thus he was a US citizen.

"Okay, Derek. No worries. Come back to Conway and we'll drive down to Nashville together and see what we can do."

It was a six hour drive each way, so I didn't get back to Nashville until the following afternoon. We bought a local newspaper and scanned the ads, looking for places I thought I could afford to share with other students, as I'd done in Conway. Ben drove us around the city while I made notes. Then we parked and walked around the Meharry campus.

In one of the buildings I noticed some students sitting in a lecture hall. Classes hadn't begun yet. They were junior medical students studying for their board exams. We opened the door as quietly as possible and sat down in seats at the very back of the room.

A wave of intense emotion swept over me as I allowed the reality to sink in that I was finally, finally where I had wanted to be when I'd left home five years earlier. My eyes flooded with tears of relief, homesickness, and gratitude for all the blessings that God and so many good people—my Samaritans—had bestowed on me along the way. I had many more miles to go before I would be practicing medicine, but that now seemed almost a cinch by comparison.

This was where I belonged and as there was no chance I was going to spend the night in that filthy apartment, and because I wouldn't think of squandering money on a hotel room, I decided to celebrate my arrival by sleeping my first night in Nashville in that lecture hall. Ben could have driven home, or even slept in his car, but he said he wanted to stay there with me and I was glad for the company.

As we sat there in the top row, looking down on the stepped rows of seats below, the lectern and blackboard at the bottom, Ben turned to look at me with tender eyes brimming with brotherly love. "Oh, man, Derek. You really made it. This is what you always wanted and here you are. I just know you're going to do well."

It was a special moment for me to be able to share with someone who knew about my journey from childhood and understood exactly how I felt. There was also in his voice a wistful note. He came to the US years before I did, as a citizen with all the advantages that citizenship afforded. He had similar ambitions but somewhere along the way he had become distracted.

When I first got to Arkansas, he was living in Atlanta enjoying the social life of a major city while allowing time for his goals to slip away. Seeing what was happening to him, I had urged, "Get out of Atlanta. Come to this tiny town in Arkansas, focus on your books, study, and get where you want to go. You won't have any peer pressure and everyone will make you feel special."

He did move to Conway to University of Central Arkansas and was on a healthcare track. Sitting there together in that medical lecture hall at Meharry, I sensed that he realized I was living his dream, that I was where he could have been, yet without all the advantages he had enjoyed. There wasn't a shred of envy or regret in his voice. He just kept saying, with shimmering eyes, "You're going to do well. You're going to do well."

That night I slept but a few winks, listening to all the

little sounds a building full of dark, empty classrooms makes in the middle of the night. When I finally heard the thump of doors opening and closing, I woke Ben and we went out to get the newspaper to begin looking for proper lodging. On our way, he had a Ghanaian brainstorm.

"You know what we should do? Take the phone book and look through it for any names that sound Ghanaian and just give them a call. Maybe someone can give us some tips or knows someone who has a place." It made perfect sense—the cultural extended family.

We crowded together into a phone booth and began flipping through the directory, starting at the beginning. Sure enough, right in the A's was a name that could be nothing but Ghanaian—Ashanti, E. On my own I would probably never have called let alone been able to carry on a conversation with a stranger, even one from Ghana. I have always struggled with shyness. But Ben had been living in the US for several years and had no such problem. He picked up the receiver, dropped in a quarter, and dialed.

"Hello! Is this the Ashanti residence? ... We are students from Ghana who have just come to town." He held the receiver between us so I could hear both sides of the conversation. He explained that I was studying medicine at Meharry and asked her where in Nashville would be the best place to find an affordable safe apartment.

When he was done, she asked, "Are you guys hungry?"

Ben looked at me, grinned, and winked. "As a matter of fact, yes."

"Where are you sleeping?"

"Well, you know, we just came to town."

"Why don't you come to me. I'll make you something to eat and we can see about the rest."

As comfortable as I had become in America, there is nothing quite so reassuring as finding in a foreign culture "your" people who are eager to help you get where you want to go. It was a great way to arrive in Nashville, meeting someone like Esi. She made us a hot home-cooked meal and we exchanged stories. She was older than we were, worked as a caterer in a hotel, and was going to marry soon. She had a wonderful, nurturing manner.

Finally, she said, "You know, this may be inappropriate, but you can see it whichever way you want. Here where I live is an area that I think you should rent. There should be apartments that are reasonable. You will need references, though. As it turns out, I have an extra room. You can stay here if you want."

Yet another Samaritan! It was a tempting offer, but I had already made arrangements to share an apartment with two other students, one from Ghana and the other from Jamaica. They were coming to Meharry from New York.

"Usually when you go to medical school," I explained, "you get to know who is in your class ahead of time and a group finds an apartment together. That way everybody understands when people are up late studying or keeping odd hours. So there are two other people who are depending on me for a place to live."

She thought in silence for a moment.

"Well, you guys will be studying a lot. Why don't all three of you crash in that room, if you want, until you find the right apartment?"

I immediately called my friends and they gave me the go-ahead. The three of us ended up living with Esi while she asked everyone she knew about available apartments. Thanks to her persistence, we soon found the perfect place at the right price. Esi became an important person in my life during my time in Nashville, joining my tribe, so to speak, and always looking out for me.

Every work day, she would stop by on her way home from her catering job to leave a package at our door of leftover banquet food. For medical students, we ate well. As internationals of color plunked down into a sometimes-hostile culture, she made us feel loved and safe. In many ways, Esi went through medical school with us. She has remained a dear friend ever since.

And thus my medical education began, with me eagerly looking forward to working on cadavers instead of carcasses.

CHAPTER 12:
FINALLY THERE

Four years after I stood in a Moscow dissection lab learning the parts of a horse, I found myself back in a dissection lab, only this time the specimen was a human being. I was twenty-six years old, four years the senior of many classmates who were fresh from earning their undergraduate degrees. Those extra four years—packed with travel, work, school, disappointments, lucky breaks, near misses, homesickness, generosity, drama, and a miracle or two—had tempered me into a young man of the world.

Nevertheless, even I felt a little light-headed on the first day of lectures when the sheet was removed from the first cadaver I had ever seen, the one my three teammates and I would be working on for the next year. The unclothed bodies, lying so still and vulnerable on the dissection tables, each had names and histories. Although we didn't know them, our professor admonished us to treat them with the same dignity we would wish to be afforded the remains of our loved ones.

"These people have donated their bodies so that you can study them. Treat them with respect. Take no pictures. Make no jokes. They have given you the opportunity to learn. Show your gratitude by not wasting a minute of it."

His words calmed my nerves. This was nothing like horses or dogs. These vessels had once held the souls of people who mattered to someone, most certainly to God. That first day was deeply spiritual on several accounts. I had officially crossed the threshold. After years of saying, "I want to be a doctor," I was becoming one. I was finally there!

Gross (meaning the total body) anatomy courses are basic training camps for future doctors and the first day is rarely without incident. Someone usually faints or becomes ill. Also, no one who has worked on a human specimen ever forgets the smell of embalming fluid. Dissection cadavers are preserved in a bath of formaldehyde, a yellowish fluid with an odor that stings the eyes and sears the nose. It gets into clothing, your skin, and even into paper. A textbook opened later at home or the library would release a whiff of formaldehyde.

For the first week or so, students tended to avoid food just before class and had no appetite after. Two weeks in and the smell had somehow faded into the background. Students were able to eat their sandwiches and snacks just outside the lab doors. You can get used to just about anything when the stakes are high.

The coursework kept us on our toes. Each day there was usually an oral exam about what we had studied the day before. It was trial by fire, good training for becoming a doctor.

During the year that it took to complete gross anatomy, each member of each team of students took turns disassembling with scalpels and other tools all the systems, organs, nerves, vessels, and tissues of the body. We also took turns making notes and sketches. We started with the head and neck, then the extremities, the nervous system, abdomen, and pelvis.

Extremities was the easiest, but only by comparison. It requires knowing where every muscle attaches and intersects with other muscle groups for each of the 206 bones in an adult human body. Head and neck are the most complex and hardest. It's the portion of an anatomy course that causes students the most grief. Those who fail it have to repeat the course, a deflating experience. Happily, it was the part I found the most fascinating.

The intricacies appealed to me. The head is the command center of the body, the communications hub, home to four of the five senses, and where we imbibe the basics of life—air, food, and water. I liked that the head and neck area is focused, contained in a small space, as opposed to the vascular, intestinal, and nerve systems, or the muscle and bone structures, that involve the whole body. You can live without a limb or certain organs, but you can't live without a head.

I had learned by this time that focusing on one thing to the exclusion of everything else was one of my natural instincts, one I had been known for among my friends and classmates in Moscow. I earned that reputation one cold winter night when I had been engaged in a serious conversation with one of my friends, an intellectual argument of some sort. We had to leave for a meeting and kept debating as we got out our boots to change into for the walk through the snow and ice. The conversation kept me absorbed during the walk and even after we arrived at our destination.

Soon after we'd left, a friend stopped by our apartment. He noticed one of my boots sitting on the floor next to one of my slippers. He knew me well enough to guess what had happened. He picked up the boot and brought it to me, laughing and shaking his head. I couldn't figure out what he was doing with it.

"Professor Egg," he said. "Did you forget what you forgot?"

I had gone out wearing a boot and a slipper.

I was equally focused at Meharry. I avoided cultivating a social life partly because of my shy nature but mostly because I was determined to make the most of my education. That meant dodging most distractions. I did have a family-away-from-family that included my roommates, who were fellow students. One was a Jamaican guy, much older than me, who wore his hair in dreadlocks, sold health tonics to help pay his way, and claimed he had worked with Bob Marley, the legendary reggae musician. The other was a Ghanaian.

There was a fourth person in my circle who became and remained a close friend. Lahar Mehta was born and raised in the States by parents who were born and raised in East Africa by parents who were born and raised in India. When Lahar was six, his father had moved the family from Chicago to Nashville to take a job as a business manager for a group of hospitals.

Lahar and I met during orientation when we happened to find ourselves in the same spot, sneaking a break from the hall where an endless parade of administrators welcomed the new class, explained policies, and assured us what wonderful experiences we were about to have. Having grown up in Nashville, Lahar knew the city well, although from the perspective of an upper-middle-class family in a good neighborhood. Lahar had chosen Meharry so he could live at home. We hit it off right away.

Lahar's coloring is light brown, like most Indians, and no one would mistake him for African. He had grown up and gone to school with mostly white kids and known little in the way of racial prejudice. In a medical school class that was about 80 percent black, 10 percent Caucasian, and 10 percent Asian, he was one of the odd men out.

Meharry was giving him quite a cultural education and the unique experience of being in the minority. We three internationals must have seemed even more exotic to him, poor as church mice with stories to tell of the many challenges we'd faced getting there. He had a car and sometimes chauffeured us to places we were too poor or too busy to get to, and then insisted on taking us home to visit his parents and filling our stomachs.

Although Lahar was an American, he understood some of the cultural challenges I faced because his father had made a similar journey, moving to America on his own, hoping to bring the rest of his family as he was able. I keenly felt that same sense of obligation and, in the years that followed, all of my siblings but one immigrated, most ending up in health-care-related professions. We were like an ant colony, linking ourselves together into a bridge so others could follow. My brother who stayed in Ghana took up and expanded the family's transportation business.

Lahar, like myself, was the eldest son in an aspiring immigrant family, a role that comes with high built-in expectations.

Our family at the graduation of my brother, Kofi Owusu (center), from Wake Forest School of Medicine in 2015. From left: Myself (Kofi Boahene), Francis, James, Mum, Kofi Owusu, Dad, Akwasi, Elaine and Yvette. Our brother George was in Ghana and unable to attend.

We were each profoundly devoted to our families. Knowing he understood me, I was able to be more open with him and discuss my dreams and frustrations.

Among my fears was concern about Meharry's future. I overheard gossip among other students who expressed a great deal of mistrust of the white medical establishment in Nashville. Meharry had been having financial trouble and there were rumors that powerful interests were angling to take over the school's W. Hubbard Hospital should the school actually fail.

The prospect of any school failing would upset its students but Meharry was a special case as one of only two traditionally black medical schools with long histories and legacies. In the national press there was a growing debate about lack of access for black students to graduate schools in professions like law and medicine. Medical schools that finished their recruiting drives without accepting a single black applicant found themselves on the defensive. In the years since, Meharry formed an alliance with Vanderbilt University and is today on an even keel. At the time, open talk that the school might lose its accreditation—which would have been a disaster—made it seem plausible.

Although we weren't Americans, when we internationals went out of our apartment we were assumed to be. Lahar eagerly showed us the better side of his home town but we had to point out telltale signs of prejudice he'd never noticed. One day we went to an ice cream store, part of a well-known chain, in Nashville's most affluent neighborhood. The other customers stared at us as we placed and waited for our orders. When I paid for my cone, the cashier, instead of putting my change in my outstretched palm, put it down on the counter.

On another occasion we were browsing for clothes in a shop in a mall when I noticed I was being followed and furtively eyed by a store clerk. "They don't do it with the others," I said. "Watch." Lahar was shocked.

He and I had grown up in very different circumstances but we shared a trait that would make us both good doctors—when someone told us our ambitions or goals were lofty or impossible, we became more committed to them. So many times I had been told, "You can't do that," but I did it anyway—getting my American visa, escaping Russia, learning to fix cars, getting my student visa, and so on.

One of the rules Meharry students were expected to abide by was not to take employment outside of school. Tuition for most of the American students was heavily subsidized. Those of us on academic visas, whose families could not contribute, had to find other sources of income.

I struggled with my finances during my second year of medical school as my savings dwindled.

I had to do something so, contrary to school policy, I took a job at a grocery store close to my apartment, working on weekends. I lived far from campus and thought none of my classmates would ever run into me shopping at that grocery store. My coworkers knew I was a student but I kept secret exactly what and where I was studying.

My job was to bake bread and decorate cakes. When I had a few minutes of down time I'd review my school work from notes that I carried in my pocket. Besides my roommates and Lahar, no one else in my class knew I was working, until one Saturday morning when I received an order to decorate a birthday cake. Using my developing hand-eye coordination skills, I executed it with expert artistry. When the customer arrived to pick it up, I was horrified to find myself face to face with the dean of my medical school.

The floor seemed to open up under me. I stuttered out a few words, then composed myself and tried to appear as casual as possible. When he left, I was convinced the dean had not recognized me. My shift ended at noon and I headed off to campus.

As my bad luck would have it, I entered the revolving doors to the medical school lobby just as the dean was leaving. He cast his gaze on me with a furrowed brow, leaving no doubt about what was going through his mind. "Hey, didn't I just buy a cake from this guy! What's he doing in my medical school?"

I acknowledged his astonished glance, lowered my head,

and charged off before he could recover and ask me any questions. The rest of that weekend I had trouble concentrating on anything except the guillotine I expected to be waiting for me on Monday morning. The first lecture of the day was medical genetics. Five minutes into the session the doors swung open and he entered. Everyone in the room snapped to attention.

He strode to the front of the hall and, standing next to the podium, methodically scanned the rows of seats until his eyes came to rest on me. He leaned toward the professor, muttered a few words, and then walked out without doing or saying anything more.

I was busted and started praying to myself that all I had been through and accomplished up to that point would not come to an end because of some cake frosting. A day passed without incident, and another and another until it became clear that I had somehow been spared. I would learn later that my file was reviewed, and because my grades were perfect and my class attendance excellent, the dean had recommended no action be taken. I continued to work at the grocery store until I completed my second year and began clinical rotations.

While I was putting my hand-eye coordination skills to good use writing "Happy Birthday" in icing, Lahar was signing up with the US Navy for service he would begin once he finished medical school. Knowing his parents would protest, he just did it and gave them the news as a fait accompli. I understood his decision to bypass the "You can't do that!" stage.

Lahar told me he thought military experience was something every American should feel obligated to have, or at least some type of social work. This made sense to me since Ghana had a national service requirement which I had fulfilled working for the meteorological service crunching data for weather forecasters. In his case, the Navy needed physicians. Once he'd completed his medical training he hoped to enter the service as an officer and receive additional training in leadership.

"And," he said winking, "the uniform is very cool."

Medical school is a four-year program with the first two years devoted mostly to classroom and lab work. Then medical students begin their rotations or clerkships in the major specialties (internal medicine, pediatrics, obstetrics and gynecology, and so on), practicing medicine in a hospital setting under supervision.

My first clinical rotation was in surgery at the Blanchfield Army Community Hospital at Fort Campbell, Kentucky, named for Colonel Florence Aby Blanchfield, superintendent of the Army Nursing Corps during World War II. I spent two weeks in the otolaryngology department doing procedures on the face, neck, and ears: removing tonsils in children, putting pressure-equalization tubes in eardrums, sinus surgery, and so on.

I had briefly thought about specializing in orthopedic surgery but changed my mind during my first week on call. On June 18, 1996, two Army helicopters collided during training maneuvers and our emergency room was suddenly full of young men with the most traumatic injuries imaginable—shattered bones poking out of open wounds, gaping wounds, blood everywhere.

Among the most vivid snapshots in my memory from that

day is watching trauma surgeons crack open the chest of a young man and directly massage his heart to revive its beat. I helped as much as I could, retracting limbs and holding pressure on bleeding wounds. Two years of medical school had not prepared me for anything like it. In the end, six soldiers died. Those who were saved faced long recoveries.

When it was over I was filled with admiration for the efforts of all those doctors, nurses, paramedics, and orderlies. But now I knew for sure that retracting broken limbs was not going to be my thing. I would stick to the head and neck—otolaryngology.

Because otolaryngology is a rigorous field and lucrative, getting accepted into the limited training programs that were available was highly competitive. Like most everything else I pursued, getting in would require a methodical approach. This included a rotation in surgical critical care at Boston University Hospital, and then an otolaryngology clerkship at Case Western Hospital in Cleveland. I wanted to learn all the basics of what to expect, the kinds of questions professors would ask a student, what kinds of behaviors they were looking for.

A few months earlier, at the end of my second year of medical school, I had received a letter from an institution in the Upper Midwest saying they had a summer program where medical students could go and observe for a couple of weeks. In the rush of things, I wrote back thanking them but turning it down because the program would end a few weeks before I was to take the US Medical Licensing Exam, a major, three-part ordeal. The score determines what specialties you are considered suitable for and which hospitals will consider hiring you.

It wasn't until two weeks later that it hit me like a bolt of lightning. The Mayo Clinic! I hadn't recognized the name but suddenly it came back to me. I had read about the Mayo Clinic in the encyclopedia my father gave me when I was about ten years old. I had been inspired and told my friends I would work there one day.

Praying that I had not just given up the opportunity of my career, I called Mayo. The woman who was organizing the program told me, "I'm so glad you called because we had one spot left and we were just about to call an alternate and give it away."

My heart soared with joy. "If you still have it, I want it."

It was another lucky break (ordained by God!) that would define my future.

CHAPTER 13:
HOW'S THE KIWI?

In my last year of medical school, 1998-99, I received an email from one of the Ghanaians who'd been a schoolmate from my Russian veterinary school days. The ripple from that email would spread and eventually bring me the greatest personal happiness I have ever experienced.

Like many Ghanaians, my friend has a non-Ashanti given name—Omega—in addition to his Ghanaian name. Why his parents chose the last letter of the Greek alphabet I never learned. Perhaps he was their last child.

My Ashanti given name is Kofi, the same as former Secretary-General of the United Nations Kofi Annan. Kofi is the name given a male child born on a Friday, the day of my birth. This is a common naming practice. I have a brother who was also born on Friday and his Ashanti name is also Kofi.

Each day of the week is said to be associated with certain personality traits. Friday's boy child is a leader. Monday's girl child is a nurturer. This system is said to have had its roots in the high infant mortality rate that prevailed during the first seven days after birth. A child would be given its name after it had survived the first week.

The naming ceremony is called an outdooring and holds great significance in Ghanaian culture. It is the first time the child is presented to the world, the extended family and the proverbial village it will take to raise it. A respected elder leads the ceremony.

The specific outdooring ritual varies from tribe to tribe, but in most cases the child is placed on the lap of the elder, who then dips a finger in water and touches the child's lip while proclaiming, "When you say it is water, it must mean water." This is repeated with something bitter, such as salty water, and something sweet. It is the symbolic preparation of the child for the challenges of life and emphasizes the importance of being true to one's word.

My parents are widely known in the missionary world as James and Helena. Many people know me by my anglicized name, Derek. I have a sister named Elaine, and five other siblings with English-sounding names. Elaine and I got ours from a popular 1960s singing duo, twin teenaged children as pink-cheeked and British as can be. Elaine and Derek Thompson had recorded an album of religious songs that my father found appealing.

Even though my sister and I are not twins—I was the oldest—my father may have been inspired by the high rate of twin births in West Africa. Maybe he was praying for twins.

The giving of English names dates to the days when Ghana was the slave-trading hub of West Africa. Ruled by the British, native family names were difficult to pronounce and spell and given names—days of the week—were so common that the British assigned recognizable English names. Over the years, as Ghanaians increasingly adopted Christianity, they and their children were baptized with their Christian-sounding names. This tradition continues today. Ghanaians are as likely as Brits or Yankees to give their children the names of movie stars or singers in addition to their traditional names.

Omega shared with me a desire to switch to medical school but, like me, he couldn't persuade the authorities. He, too, went to the American embassy in Moscow and managed to get a visa to visit America. Unlike me, he stayed in Russia.

"It's the fear of the unknown," he explained. "I don't know anybody in the States. I don't know what I would be doing when I got there. I'm not happy with what I'm doing here, but it's half a loaf."

When I prepared to leave Russia for the last time, he was the only person who knew about it and went with me to the train station where we bid each other an emotional farewell. Although we had not grown up in the same neighborhood, having first met in Russia, he was the type of friend who, as we say in Ghana, would help push you up a tree to get the fruit.

When I was settled in Arkansas with the Lennon family, he gathered up all my winter gear and other things I'd left behind and mailed it all to me. He also obtained documents, transcripts, and other records I needed for my college applications.

Omega graduated from veterinary school and left Russia in 1996, but not before he became a victim of hooliganism against foreigners, Africans in particular. He was at a train station waiting for a bus when a group of skinheads chased and beat him, in broad daylight. No one tried to intercede but an American tourist on the bus told him he had a serious wound on the back of his head and warned him not to fall asleep, in case he had a concussion. When I heard about it I regretted not trying harder to convince him to leave with me.

Omega ended up practicing veterinary medicine in New Zealand, where one of his brothers lived. We stayed in touch and one day, in my last year of medical school, he phoned with a mysterious question.

"Kofi, do you remember we had a conversation while we were in Moscow, about an argument you were making?"

That had been seven years earlier. I had no idea what he was talking about.

"You remember," he said. "We were talking about your faith, Christianity, and about why you were waiting for marriage. I told you I knew someone who felt the same way, but I never mentioned who it was."

I had a vague recollection, but not much more.

"Well, the person I was referring to lives here in New Zealand," he said, his voice rising with excitement. "And you need to talk to her."

"Her?"

Okay, I thought. There is a girl he thought I might be interested in. It seemed at times as though Omega's main mission in life was trying to figure out how to get me married. He teased me about being shy with women and he and some other classmates were betting I would at least have a Russian girlfriend, or maybe even marry a Russian.

However, I remained deaf to the sirens' calls. First, I didn't socialize the way my friends did, at parties. I didn't drink alcohol. I had made a commitment to remain celibate until I was married and I had no inner turmoil about it. It was, for me, the only way and thus easy to accept.

Nevertheless, Omega and others—baffled by my intransigence—tried to tempt me. Once he tried to get me interested in one of our lecturers, a particularly beautiful woman who communicated her interest by being a bit flirtatious.

"Don't you realize she really, really likes you," Omega pleaded. "You're a good student, different—she likes that."

"Okay, that's great." I shrugged. "So?"

"Well, what are you going to do about it?"

"What do you mean? She likes me, so fine. That's just not me. That's not how I was raised."

"You wait," Omega would say, exasperated. "That's what everybody says. Just wait."

I had nothing against Russian women. It was the kind of relationships they would have before marriage that, raised as a Christian, was out of the question.

The same pity was heaped on me when I was studying in Arkansas. There was a very attractive and popular girl I was tutoring in chemistry who my friends assured me was interested. "She really likes you."

"That's too bad." Once again, I just shrugged.

"What do you mean? You say you want to get married but how can you if you're not going to date anybody?"

"I will know the person I'm to marry the minute we meet."

"How do you know that?"

"Because God has a plan for me and that's part of the plan. I will know her when I meet her and so far I haven't."

"How can you know He has a plan? Does God speak to you?" In general, Ghanaians are ardent Christians and it's doubtful I would have found myself in such a conversation at home. But far away, in a diverse, casual culture full of opportunity like America, many Africans I met found it easier and more exciting to adapt.

"I have faith that if I make good choices God will guide me. I know because my mum has been praying for this all her life."

My friends in Arkansas would throw their hands up, as exasperated and baffled as Omega had been. I couldn't blame them for not understanding how profound an influence my mother was, in ways that were demonstrative as well as subtle. Being the oldest child, I would be the first of my siblings to wake up. In the pre-dawn darkness, when the stillness was broken only by the occasional crow of a nearby rooster, the only sound was my mother's muffled voice coming from my parents' bedroom. Every morning she prayed for me and my siblings.

"God, I pray for my sons, that they will do well. Please give them wisdom as they grow up to make the right choices, to marry someone compatible and faithful."

The sound of her prayers became as familiar to me as the sound of her beating heart when I'd rest my head on her breast. Along with the Bible studies we kids did with my father at home and the Sunday school classes we attended, her prayers have served as a beacon through thick and thin. All these years later, it is still hard sometimes to talk about it without strong feelings of love, gratitude, and admiration.

Omega's enthusiasm about this stranger was premature—a girl I had never met, about whom I knew nothing, and who lived half a world away?

"Okay, Omega." I appreciated his trying to push me up the fruit tree, so I indulged him without much consideration.

"Can I give you her email?"

"Sure." That was it. I wrote down the address and, distracted by the demands of my studies and other obligations, forgot the conversation.

Two weeks later, Omega sent a scolding email.

"That person I mentioned said you haven't emailed her."

Feeling foolish, I wrote her an email.

"My friend said we share the same views. Maybe we should talk sometime."

Thus began a friendship that evolved into a global courtship, by telephone, email, and finally by jet. Her name was Adjoa—Monday's child, the nurturer. Her anglicized name was Ruth. She was studying dental surgery at the University of Otago in Dunedin, New Zealand.

I didn't know it at the time, but Omega had himself been trying to court Adjoa for nearly two years. She rebuffed him at every turn and he had finally given up. Then he realized that she and I would be a good match.

Adjoa, like myself, wasn't looking for a spouse but believed she would know that person when she met him. In the meantime, she felt no urgency about finding a life mate. She had been deeply affected by the sorrow and despair she saw in her peers who had made lifelong commitments before they were ready. She was determined to avoid making that mistake.

"That's not going to be me," she told Omega. "I'm not going to give myself to somebody to allow them to walk over me. I've seen it in people's lives. They did not recover."

Even if Adjoa had been looking, Omega disagreed with her on too many important aspects of life, faith, philosophy—topics they'd discussed and debated for hours. After Omega gave up his romantic campaign, they remained good friends. One day, during one of their discussions, Omega casually mentioned, "I think I've had this conversation before with somebody, but I can't remember who."

A few weeks later, at a party, he told Adjoa, "You know, there is somebody I want you to meet."

"Who? Why?" Adjoa thought it must be a joke or a trick.

"He's a friend of mine. He's studying to be a doctor in America. He's a guy who I've had conversations with that were similar to ours."

Adjoa was about to earn her degree and begin doing what she wanted, quite happy without feeling the need for anyone to help push her up the fruit tree. When Omega gave her my email address and suggested she write, she scoffed at him.

"What? Write an email to a complete stranger to amuse you? No, I'm not doing that."

"Okay. Can I at least give him your email address?"

"Okay. I don't care." She shrugged. "Nothing will ever come of it."

Afterward, Adjoa and her closest friend had a good laugh at Omega's foolishness. Her friend said, giggling, "Wouldn't it be funny if you ended up marrying the guy?"

In our first few exchanges and phone calls, Adjoa and I immediately had something very tangible and important in common. Each of us had chosen a career in healthcare and each had chosen to specialize in the same part of the body. We were linked by our knowledge of human anatomy and health.

Adjoa's inspiration was a film she'd seen about Mercy Ships, a nonprofit that operates the largest non-governmental hospital ship in the world. The current vessel, the *Africa Mercy*, travels from port to port, dropping anchor and spending up to a year providing sophisticated health services to the poorest of the world's poor.

My inspiration started with an encyclopedia entry about the Mayo Clinic. My goal to give back to my fellow Ghanaians was born the day one of my schoolmates nearly bled to death of injuries from a motorbike accident while waiting for care in an understaffed emergency room.

We shared a commitment to use our skills to bring care to those who lacked access, although she said she was glad she wouldn't have to operate on someone's arteries or remove a tumor.

"I like dental surgery because it's artistic. I don't think I could express myself so much in medicine as I would be able to in dentistry."

We swapped family histories, a matter of great interest to people from small nations like ours. It can sometimes seem as if everyone has heard of, knows, or is related to everyone else. In America you might go so far as to order a background check for a prospective son- or daughter-in-law. In Ghana, you just ask some relatives and friends until you find someone who knows, and may be related.

Adjoa's granduncle had been a doctor. Her father followed in his footsteps and her mother was a midwife. When she was very young the family moved from Ghana to Edinburgh, Scotland, so her father could earn his master's degree in public health. They later spent time in the US and after that he taught medicine and conducted research in Nigeria and elsewhere.

Adjoa's parents had always intended to return the family to Ghana but each time the opportunity arose conditions were unstable. In the end they decided the Ghanaian school system wouldn't be able to provide her and her brother with the rigorous sciences and maths education they would need to follow in their parents' footsteps.

After a stint in Papua New Guinea, they settled in New Zealand when Adjoa was ten years old. She attended an international secondary school with American and Australian teachers and lost her native accent. People often mistake her for American-born.

Omega had been right. Adjoa and I had much in common, especially as it related to faith and family. Her family, like mine, often prayed together and, like me, she often heard her parents praying in their room. Music was also important.

"My dad taught himself how to play the bass guitar," she told me. "He sings harmony and I would often hear them singing and praying together. At least once a week, if not more, we'd all pray together."

We shared a strong belief in remaining chaste until marriage.

"My mother never really said, 'Do this or that,' or 'don't do this or that'. They mostly parented by example."

Eventually we agreed to tell our families that love appeared to be in the air, allowing them to inquire into each other's background before giving their blessing. Not only did our families pass inspection, but the process unearthed an improbable and beautiful connection.

Before she became pregnant with me, my mother had experienced several complicated pregnancies that ended in stillbirths. The family wanted her to have the best care the next time around so they sought out a noted obstetrician who delivered me safe and sound. That obstetrician was Adjoa's granduncle!

This was profound evidence of God's handiwork. We'd been connected to each other's families since our births.

When my long-distance courtship with Adjoa began, I kept it to myself. Lahar began to notice that I was spending multiple late nights in the computer lab, my only access to email. When he asked what I was up to I made up some excuse. But he was relentlessly suspicious. I finally capitulated and confessed that I was in correspondence with somebody that was of Ghanaian descent who lived in New Zealand.

Lahar told our third roommate and then began the nightly teasing when I came home late.

"So, Kofi, how's the kiwi? Do you even know what she looks like?"

I would just smile.

CHAPTER 14:
GONE, GONE, GONE!

When I first "met" Adjoa through email and then by phone, we were each completing our final year of medical training and looking forward to beginning the next phase of our professional lives. She would be going to Andover, England, for a one-year commitment in the National Health Service. I was going to begin my residency training.

My future was falling into place about as well as anyone could have hoped, prayed, and worked for. The previous year I had been granted a surgical clerkship in a program at the Mayo Clinic in Rochester, Minnesota, spending one month learning and performing head and neck surgeries. The people I worked with were always surprised and amused to learn that I had started my training in veterinary medicine, in Russia no less. I became known as the only surgeon "qualified to operate on anything that moves, animal or human."

My first time at Mayo had been the month I spent there observing during my second summer break. The one-month surgery clerkship had been in the dead of winter. When people at Meharry learned I was going to Minnesota, the first thing many said was, "My goodness! All that snow, and so cold!"

"It can't be more snow than I saw in Moscow!" Snow and cold were minor inconveniences to someone who had first dreamed about working at the Mayo Clinic when he was ten years old and lived half the globe away.

The next milestone was to graduate from medical school and begin a residency program in otolaryngology, a specialty that is as complex and competitive as neurological (brain and nervous system) surgery, with an equally limited number of open positions each year at the top institutions. Being offered a residency in any specialty anywhere in the US is a highly competitive process.

Each year more than 30,000 medical school students, about half from the US and the other half from around the world, apply to a central registry—the National Resident Matching Program. The Match, as it is known, uses a variety of factors to identify students who have indicated preferred specialties with appropriate institutions looking for potential applicants to interview. The results of this process are announced on one day—Match Day, in March of the fourth year of medical school—when students learn if and where they will be launching their careers.

There was only one specialty I wanted and only one place I wanted to go—the Mayo Clinic. Because I had laid the groundwork, earned good scores, and was on track to graduate first in my class, and because the Mayo professors and residents had had a chance to see me at work, I was invited for an interview. Besides Mayo, I interviewed at six other hospitals. I matched at Mayo. I was in! For the next five years I would be a surgeon at one of the most respected medical and research institutions in the world.

It was a big moment for Meharry as well. The school was coming back from a financial and accreditation crisis a few years earlier. My acceptance at Mayo, in such a coveted specialty, was a feather in the school's cap. I was the second Meharry graduate in two years to go on to Mayo for a surgical residency, adding to Meharry's improving reputation.

Graduation takes place each year in September. Mine was in 1999, nine years since that hard day when my parents drove me to the airport in Accra for my flight to Moscow.

It had also been nine years since I'd seen my beloved mother, who I knew had started every day of all those years praying quietly in the pre-dawn darkness for me to make good choices and for God to guide and watch over me. I had missed my family every day of those nine years. Now, finally, I had arranged for them to come to Meharry to share this big moment in all our lives—a moment of accomplishment, thanksgiving, and love. My sister and two of my brothers were coming as well.

Because their travel schedules and the preparations for the ceremony overlapped, there was only a brief few minutes when I was able to greet my mother and father, and Cindy and Joe Lennon—my American family—beforehand.

At some point during my time in Arkansas and Nashville, my mother had sent Cindy a typical Ghanaian dress in the Pan-African colors—red, yellow, and green. Cindy thought it would be fun to wear it to my graduation. She remembered thinking at the time that my mother might have a similar instinct, and she was right.

"There we were," Cindy said later. "I'm white and all dressed up like I was African. Derek's mother, black as ebony, was wearing a beautiful Western dress, all white. When we first met we both burst out laughing."

Mum and Cindy at my medical school graduation.

People often tell me that I appear calm no matter what's going on around me. That day, on the inside at least, I was overflowing with emotion. I reached back to my childhood for inspiration for how best to express what I felt when it was my turn to step up on the stage, shake the hand of the dean, and receive my degree with those beautiful words hand-inscribed: Kofi Derek Owusu Boahene, M.D.

As I nervously joked with my classmates, donning our caps and gowns, receiving our final instructions, I remembered my dad's techniques for motivating us kids to work hard and do well. When I was about eight years old I asked him if he could buy me a real, professional soccer ball, not like the smaller training balls that we used at school.

"You can have your soccer ball, if," he said, "at the end of this semester you are one of the top three students in your class."

We received our report cards on the last day of the semester and the headmaster posted the rankings on the bulletin board in the hallway. I joined the mob of boys crowding and jostling to see how they'd done. My heart leaped when I saw my name at the very top. I ran nonstop the nearly three miles from school to home, shouting "Me kɔ! Me kɔ! Me kɔ!" Pronounced *mi kor*, the Ashanti words translate literally as "I'm gone," but to me meant, "I did it!" I abandoned my naturally shy demeanor and burst into our house. "I'm gone! I'm gone! I'm gone!"

"What's all this yelling?" My mother came out from the kitchen, eyeing me with furrowed brow as she dried her hands on her apron. "Where have you gone?"

"I'm gone! I'm gone! I'm gone!"

I proudly showed her my report card. My father was away on business but some uncles who lived with us managed to get him on the phone.

"James, your son is going crazy. He has been yelling he's 'gone, gone, gone,' but nobody knows where he's gone to."

When Father finally returned, I greeted him at the door with my report card and quietly beamed as he reviewed it and then said, "Very well done, son."

The next morning I awoke to find a bright new professional soccer ball next to my pillow. My outburst of joy became part of my personal lore within the family: Remember the time Derek went crazy and said he was gone?

So that day at Meharry in September 1999, when the dean called out my name to come forward and receive my diploma, I took the scroll, held it over my head, and with my eyes flooding and a lump in my throat, yelled out the Ashanti words—"Me kɔ! Me kɔ! Me kɔ!" It was the proudest day of my life.

CHAPTER 15:
IN THE FOOTSTEPS
OF GIANTS

When I was first admitted to medical school in 1994, I could not get a student loan on my own or even qualify for a credit card. Just a few days after my graduation in 1999, with student loans to pay and my career not yet begun, my mailbox suddenly sprouted a cornucopia of unsolicited loan and credit card offers.

There is a saying in my native language, Akan, that poses a rhetorical question: Because we are going to die someday, should we not sleep? Why concern ourselves with the future when we know the end result of life is death?

As tempting as it was to live for the moment and spoil myself with some of this bounty pouring out of my mailbox, medical training is a long journey with graduation being just one mile marker of many. I learned early on to stay disciplined and accept that gratification would have to be deferred.

My financial interest was in paying off as quickly as possible the student loan that Dr. Manion, my chemistry professor, and Dennis Willis, the nurse from my church, had guaranteed. I also wanted to send some money home to help my parents and provide opportunities for my younger siblings. So the snazzy new car would have to wait.

Instead, I bought a used car with high miles that my mechanic's eye found to be solid, packed up my few belongings, and headed off on Interstate 65 toward Minnesota to begin my residency training at Mayo. With me was Ebenezer, my childhood friend from Ghana who had applied to schools in Sweden when I did and ended up studying and settling in Stockholm. He came to visit and help celebrate my success.

Ebenezer had earned a degree in chemical engineering, gotten married and had a little girl. The trip was wonderfully nostalgic and after nine years apart we had plenty of stories to share.

How different things would have been, I thought, had that letter I needed—so I could go to Sweden—arrived a day before I flew off to Moscow. "Kofi, whatever God has arranged for you, no man can take away." Those had been the guiding words of my grandmother and I believed that the path God had arranged for me included my time in Russia, even though it felt like a detour.

Looking back on it now, I cherish that experience. It enriched my life and broadened my perspectives in many ways. If only Grannie had been around to see her predictions come true, but she died at 103 years old while I was abroad.

Our drive to Minnesota took us through Lafayette, Indiana, where we visited with another Russian school mate, Victoria. We first met at the airport in Accra when we boarded that chartered flight to Moscow. Her mother had singled me out of the crowd and asked me to look out for her daughter. I was honored to be asked and took that responsibility seriously. But when I teased her about it later, she insisted that *my* mother had asked *her* to look out for *me*. Our friendship blossomed and we became as close as siblings without actually being related.

"Vic" and I were assigned to Krasnodar for our first year studies, and later to Moscow where we continued our veterinary training. She was in the room and witnessed the time the authorities whisked me away in a windowless van to be quarantined in a remote hospital.

It had been seven years since we'd seen each other, so we also had a lot to talk about. After completing her veterinary degree she enrolled in a post-graduate training program in veterinary pathology at Purdue University. As fate would have it, Victoria later pursued her PhD at Johns Hopkins and I was present as a faculty member when she defended her doctoral dissertation. She now heads a veterinary diagnostic lab in Shanghai.

The drive to Rochester with all of the reminiscing was a perfect transition to the next step in my journey. Rochester is the third largest city in Minnesota, home to IBM, the Mayo Clinic, and Assisi Heights Spirituality Center, the motherhouse of the Sisters of St. Francis.

The Mayo Clinic started out in 1889 as a family practice established by a doctor—William W. Mayo—and his two sons who had also become doctors. The inspiration to build a hospital was a tornado that destroyed a third of the city in 1883. The Sisters of St. Francis worked with the Mayos to provide facilities and care for the many who were injured.

That collaboration was the spark for St. Mary's Hospital, named for the nun who led the order, which in turn grew into the world's first, and now largest, integrated nonprofit medical group practice in the world. Today the Mayo Clinic has 4,000 doctors on staff and more than 50,000 employees.

It had been many years since that day I stumbled on the Mayo entry in an encyclopedia and the dream I was about to fulfill was born. I was walking in the footsteps of giants and more inspired than ever to encourage my brothers to also study medicine. I thought that perhaps, one day, we would become the Mayos of Ghana and open a group practice. But before that could happen, I had to train to be become a competent surgeon.

Residency training in otolaryngology—head and neck surgery—takes five years and begins with a year of general surgery, the equivalent of an internship when medical students transition from being observers to being busy, vigorous, observant medical professionals. Just like the stereotype, at Mayo we interns worked long hours and were expected to know everything about every patient, right down to the frequency and consistency of their bowel movements.

I started my internship year rotating through the otolaryngology service; a good transition from being a medical student since it was the surgical subspecialty I was most familiar with. The otolaryngologist is frequently the first responder for medical emergencies involving the head region, especially when a patient stops breathing. I hoped my first night on call would be relatively calm, to give me a chance to familiarize myself with the routine.

That, however, was not to be. My first page came in at about 9 o'clock. A patient was coughing up blood. Depending on what the cause was, he could potentially bleed to death in minutes. The man had throat cancer and had had his larynx removed two weeks earlier. He was able to breathe through a permanent hole that had been surgically created in his neck. I quickly placed a breathing tube through the hole and inflated an attached cuff to seal off his trachea and prevent the blood from flooding his lungs. The bleeding appeared to stop but we needed to find the source.

With the senior resident called in, we rushed him to radiology where a dye was injected into his blood stream. The x-ray scans relieved our fear that it was his carotid artery, the main artery that supplies the brain. He was lucky. The bleeding was from a smaller vessel in the neck, which we easily controlled. My residency had begun with a bang.

Before formal training programs for surgery existed, surgeons learned by travelling from place to place to study as apprentices under established master surgeons. This style of training has mostly been replaced around the world, but not at the Mayo Clinic. My second year of training was a series of such apprenticeships. Every three months I worked directly with a different senior surgeon. I saw every patient they saw and assisted on every surgery they performed. I found this style of training suited me well.

The case that helped define my future subspecialty began with a call to consult on a newborn who had been transferred to our hospital from another. Among other abnormalities, this child was born with no nose, just a small stump of fleshy tissue, a condition called proboscis lateralis.

We designed a surgical technique to create a nose and this child became my patient for the next four years as we continued to refine the structure until he had a nearly normal-looking nose. It was a satisfying outcome and one that attracted enough attention that I was invited to publish the clinical description of the surgical repair in a medical journal. If I had any doubts about facial reconstructive surgery, that child erased them once and for all.

CHAPTER 16:
ON A PINK CLOUD

Once I was settled at the Mayo Clinic, Adjoa and I reached the point in our long-distance courtship that we wanted to meet. Although I had become a working surgeon, earning a modest living, I was still in the US on a student visa and could not just leave the country—even to visit Ghana—and be certain I'd be readmitted.

Since I dared not leave, I suggested she apply to do a one-month rotation at Mayo. There was no guarantee she'd get it, but in spite of the competition she was accepted into the oral maxillofacial (jawbone) surgery service.

We had been communicating regularly for nearly a year or so, and had exchanged photos, but the true test of whether we were a match would come when we finally met. My confidence was high but still it was a nerve-racking wait at the little airport in Rochester, Minnesota, for her final connecting flight from Minneapolis—the end of a long, six-legged journey that had started in New Zealand.

She emerged from the exit door wearing a blue top, black pants, and boots. The instant I saw her I knew we would marry.

Adjoa's month at Mayo was no holiday for either of us. She was working long hours and I was always on call. What time we had to spend together was brief and typically on a bench somewhere on the hospital campus. As a junior resident I practically lived at the hospital. We would try each day to meet for lunch and talk until, inevitably, I'd be paged and have to go back to my patients.

The month flew by. When I bid her goodbye at the airport, we knew we were meant to be together, but I had not yet proposed. There remained obstacles, chief among them my visa status. We planned another visit of several weeks during the winter months.

By this time, Adjoa expected a proposal but I wanted to try to surprise her at least a little. Instead of an expensive candlelit dinner I could not afford, or bending on one knee in front of a roomful of people who weren't our families, I put the modest engagement ring I'd bought in the cargo pocket of my pants one day and went to meet her with my hands purposely full of books.

"You know, I think I forgot something I need," I said. "It should be in my pocket. Could you check, and get it out for me?" She retrieved the ring and broke into a wide, blushing grin.

We began planning our wedding faced with a major decision—where? Because she could travel without worry, we discussed marrying in the States. The proper venue would have been in New Zealand where her family lived and where she had a circle of close friends, including our mutual friend and matchmaker, Omega. It might be another three years or so before I'd be finished at Mayo and my visa status would be resolved.

So after Adjoa returned home I investigated and found that I could visit Canada or Mexico as a tourist on my non-immigrant visa and come back without a problem. I realized that if I went to either country I could visit a US consulate there and formally apply to get my status changed. If I could replace the student visa in my passport to a work visa, I could get written advance permission from the Immigration Service to go to New Zealand knowing I could re-enter.

There was risk in applying. Once my application had been reviewed at the consulate, the clerk would have to stamp the decision in my passport. If the application was denied, I would likely be prevented from re-entering the US and would once again face the prospect of having to return to Russia or go home to Ghana and start the visa process all over again. That could end my Mayo internship. At least it would cause a significant interruption. The stakes couldn't have been higher.

I wrestled with what to do. I prayed about it, and then prayed some more. I consulted several immigration lawyers and showed them all my paperwork.

"Do I have everything right?"

"Yes," they said. "You have everything you need. You should have no problem."

Feeling confident, but without mentioning it to Adjoa— I didn't want to alarm her—I booked a flight to El Paso,

Texas, and crossed the border the next morning to Ciudad Juárez, Mexico, just across the Rio Grande. It was the least expensive destination with a full-time consulate.

With my portfolio of documents and my application I made my way to the consulate, located in an ordinary part of the city across from auto repair shops and the like. Once inside, I anxiously waited in line in the visa section. The line inched forward until there was only one person ahead of me. I watched the clerk as she reviewed his application and then my stomach flip-flopped when she shook her head and stamped his passport. Denied! For just a moment, I considered fleeing and going back to Minnesota. Maybe I had come on a bad day. Maybe there was a quota that had been filled already. I said one last prayer and stepped forward.

Once again, as I had in Moscow, I found myself across a desk from a young State Department clerk, explaining my rather complicated history—a Ghanaian passport with a visitor's visa granted in Russia a decade earlier and altered to a student visa years later. The clerk reviewed all my paperwork and told me, "Well it looks like you've got all your papers in order."

I felt a flicker of relief before she added, "But because your first entry into the US was not from Ghana, we can't issue you a work visa from this embassy. You'll have to return to your home country or where you got your student visa and apply at the embassy there."

As calmly as I could manage, a lump rising in my throat, I explained that I was a doctor and that I was doing my internship in the United States, that it was a multi-year program, that I had been working and that my visa was now work-related.

"Maybe you have heard of it. I work at the Mayo Clinic."

She shook her head and shrugged as she reached for a stamp. "I'm sorry. It's just the way the rules are."

Just then, a woman who had been walking behind the clerk's desk suddenly stopped and backed up. She exchanged a few words of Spanish with the clerk. Then she looked at me.

"The Mayo Clinic? You work at the Mayo Clinic?"

"Yes!" I said. "You've heard of it?"

"Oh, I love that place!" A big, beautiful smile spread across her face. "My mother was there when she was sick. It's just the best hospital in the world. There's this museum there, and ... Which department do you work in?"

"Otolaryngology," I said. "Ear, nose, and throat. Who took care of your mother?"

She remembered the name.

"Yes, I know him. Very nice guy."

"Yeah," she said. "I really do just love that place. In fact, I'm taking my mother for a follow-up soon. So, how can we help you?"

My heart was rollercoastering as I recounted my dilemma.

"Let me take a look at this paperwork." The clerk handed her my folder and the woman took a moment to flip through the pages, nodding her head once or twice. Then she handed it back to the clerk.

"Listen, this guy is legit. Everything's fine. Just give him the visa stamp."

It was hard to control the urge to jump up and hug her.

"Well, see you at Mayo, maybe!"

She chuckled then disappeared as quickly and casually as she had arrived, before I could properly thank her. The clerk dispassionately stamped my passport, handed it back to me, and called out, "Next!"

I finally could take a full breath—and say a prayer of gratitude. I left holding my passport tight in my hand, floating on a pink cloud of happiness.

To this day, I wonder who that woman was because I have always wanted to thank her. I'm certain she had no idea the enormous impact of what she did, nor the serendipity of how it happened. Had the person before me taken a few extra seconds, she might not have been walking by and been close enough to hear the words "Mayo Clinic." As opposed to serendipity or luck, I regarded that fortuitous instant in time as another bit of proof that God was watching over me and that Adjoa and I had been brought together by our faith in Him.

When I returned to Rochester, there was one more hoop to jump through. I had to apply to US Immigration to get written permission to travel to New Zealand, and to swear that I intended to come back. I had to apply for a document—oddly called an Advance Parole—that would allow me to re-enter the US after traveling abroad. I got the permission I needed and was granted a two-week vacation from work. We planned our wedding in earnest.

I had never been to New Zealand but had seen the *Lord Of The Rings* trilogy and was eager to experience that beautiful countryside in person. Being a rugby fan, I also knew of the prowess of the New Zealand All Blacks, the national team that was famous for performing an enchanting pre-game dance known as the Haka that was supposed to hypnotize and terrify opponents. And I looked forward to meeting my in-laws for the first time.

Traditional marriage in Africa is an elaborate cultural experience filled with customs and rites performed by both sides of the family. A common custom is the payment of a bride price, a gift to the family of the bride-to-be that can take the form of money, gold, cattle, land, or other property. I had no cattle or land so I was relieved that ours would be a less traditional ceremony in Wellington, thousands of miles removed from the cultural imperatives we would have faced in Ghana. My sole and poignant regret was that my parents could not make the trip. However, my sister Elaine and her husband did fly in from Chicago to witness and celebrate this important step in my life.

The ceremony was simple and quite untraditional—the bride and her party arrived in a vintage 1964 Rolls Royce Silver Cloud. We exchanged our vows, with me promising to endow Adjoa with my earthly possessions, all of which could probably have fit in a cardboard box at that point.

We honeymooned for a week along the coast of the North and South Islands and then returned to Otago for Adjoa's graduation ceremony from dental school. The next day I flew back to the States to resume my training while Adjoa stayed behind to prepare for her assignment in England. The next year would prove challenging—newlyweds living and working on two continents with our families far away.

CHAPTER 17:
ODE TO THE CHIEFS

The ancient Greek physician Hippocrates, considered the father of Western medicine, once observed that "Life is short, and art (or craft) is long." Scholars have since interpreted the meaning as expressing the idea that it takes a long time to perfect one's expertise. Nearly 2,400 years later, I can personally attest to his wisdom.

In modern times, Hippocrates's concept has been updated by, among others, Pope Paul VI (1963–1978) who once said, "In youth the days are short and the years are long. In old age the years are short and days long."

That expresses how I felt about my residency training at Mayo. When I started my internship year, the days seemed endless but looking back, the years seemed to have sped by as I accumulated a bounty of experience taking care of patients with a broad range of disease processes.

One of the more important people in my career development at Mayo and still a dear friend is Dr. Anthony Brissett, who was a second-year resident in the otolaryngology department when we first met. Born in Canada to Jamaican parents, he had studied in Canada and the States before joining Mayo.

Superficially we would seem to have been destined to click because he was the only other black resident in the department. But there was much more to it. He is a natural teacher and a colorful and exuberant motivator. Throughout our training he would often say to me, "Kofi, I know you can do this surgery. Now all you have to do is look good doing it."

Some young surgeons, after learning a new procedure, will brag about how fast they can perform it, as if it's a sports competition. "I can take tonsils out in ten minutes."

"Good is good and fast is fast, but fast is not necessarily good," Anthony cautioned. He explained that a surgery should proceed effortlessly, smoothly, with a confident but humble hand.

After our training at Mayo, Anthony joined me on a medical mission trip to Kumasi, Ghana. We worked twelve-hour days correcting lip defects, fixing fractures, and removing tumors in the same city where I had attended boarding school. And we worked in the same hospital where my schoolmates and I carried our bleeding friend after his motorbike accident.

It was Anthony's first time in Africa and I wanted him to see more than the inside of an operating theater. Some nights, when the roads were deserted, we'd hire a taxi and take a tour of the city. Jamaican by heritage, he had a strong affection for and interest in Africa and Africana. He had collected and studied African art and knew more about the continent than I.

Kumasi is the capital of the Ashanti Kingdom and home to the Ashanti king, Otumfuo Nana Osei Tutu II. He had heard about the work we were doing at the hospital and invited us to meet him at the palace. It was an entirely new and thrilling experience. In the Ashanti tradition, the king addressed me as "grandchild." He congratulated me on returning to the source of my stream to give back to my community. After that, Anthony said was convinced he had Ashanti ancestors.

Years later, he reciprocated, introducing me to Jamaica and the town where his father was born and lived before moving to Canada. The people, sounds, and smells were quite familiar to me. Even some of the words were similar to those in the native Ghanaian language. Hundreds of years after the last slaves settled in Jamaica, their descendants had retained many of their African customs and culture. The stream never forgets its source, often in subconscious ways.

In 2003 I became a chief resident and instructor at the Mayo Medical School, a yearlong position during which I was responsible for my own patients as well as teaching junior residents and medical students. As a young doctor just spreading my wings, my first case was challenging. A five-year-old Amish girl had a tumor so massive it had consumed her entire lower jaw. It had reached the point that it was interfering with her ability to breath.

Her family brought her to the emergency room in the middle of the night and I was called in to figure out how best to treat her. I decided we needed to operate right away. I performed a tracheostomy, making a surgical opening through her neck into her windpipe and inserting a temporary breathing tube to bypass the tumorous obstruction.

The biopsy results were a relief—the tumor was benign and unlikely to end her life. But the treatment would require removing her entire lower jaw and replacing it with healthy bone tissue harvested from her leg. I had participated in this type of surgery many times on adults, but never on such a young child.

The orthopedic surgeons we consulted assured us that removing a piece of bone from the child's leg was unlikely to limit her long-term growth. So with the help of one of my mentors, we removed the tumor, harvested the fibula, and used that bone tissue to completely build her a new jaw bone. The procedure was a success and I have since performed a number of similar jaw reconstructions in children, some as young as two years old.

By the end of my five years of residency, I had become a seasoned Mayo Clinic surgeon. At the graduation ceremony, the chairman of the Otorhinolaryngology Department, Dr. Charles W. Beatty, read a short poem mentioning each of the graduating chief residents, a tradition he's kept for many years.

Here is what he wrote about me and recited June 6, 2004:

Ode to the Chiefs

Well once again it's that time of the year
When our Chiefs begin to disappear.
Their houses sold and rotations through
With new jobs and mortgages to pursue.
But before they leave let's pause to reflect
On this group so interesting and select.
First we had a resident known as Derek Boahene,
But it was Kofi Boahene who came to the scene.
From somewhere East, he was our first Ghanaian.
That he quickly fit in goes without sayin'.
You could explain to him once how to perform a task
And the next time he had done even more than you asked.
He was a quick study with a cheerful smile
And an elusive wife for quite awhile.
Who was this dentist, Adjoa, his spouse?
And did he ever let her out of the house?
Finally, we met her, those who sought her
And their lives center on Akuah, their daughter.
Kofi heads north with Dr. Hilger to do Plastics.
No doubt his career will turn out fantastic.

At the end of my training I was selected as the recipient of the Distinguished Mayo Brothers Fellowship Award. This singular honor meant a great deal to me, the tiny African boy who had randomly flipped through the pages of an encyclopedia and read about the Mayo family clinic.

My heart overflowed with gratitude and with humility. I was following in the paths of giants and learning to walk like them, first my father, and now the Mayos.

After a short training trip to Adelaide, Australia, for complex cranial surgery, I returned to the States and moved our growing family to Edina, Minnesota to start my one year of fellowship training in facial plastic surgery, the final leg of a long, improbable journey.

CHAPTER 18:
THE LEAST AMONG US

By the time I had completed my five years of residency at The Mayo Clinic, plus a one-year fellowship, I had become a member of a network of professional friendships that today spans the globe. It includes a high percentage of doctors who were, and remain, involved in the medical missionary movement.

Not all of us are Christians, but all subscribe to the aspiration expressed in the Bible to remain humble regardless of our accomplishments or position, and to show tenderness for "the least among us." That includes at home as well as abroad.

My first opportunity to participate in medical missions came during my fourth year of training. One of my surgery mentors at Mayo, Dr. Eric Moore, invited me to join him and a group of other surgeons and nurses in the Mexican state of Oaxaca, a mountainous, sparsely populated province in the Pacific southwest of the country. The capital city sits on a high plateau with a climate described as eternal spring. The region is known as the most ethnically diverse of the country's thirty-one states. The two largest linguistic groups are the Zapotec and Mixtec Indians, whose cultures are believed to be 2,000 or more years old.

Among the mountain dwellers there is a birth defect called microtia that is many times more common there than anywhere else—children born with a partially formed or nonexistent external ear. Our mission focus was to build ears for these children. The procedure begins with harvesting a piece of cartilage from a rib and artistically sculpting it into the shape of an ear. The sculpted cartilage is then buried under the skin where the ear should have developed. Over several months the skin shrinks around the sculpted cartilage to form a natural-looking ear.

Artistic instincts, a good eye, and a steady hand are highly prized among otolaryngology surgeons, so much so that beginning in the 1980s applicants for residencies at leading institutions like Mayo have been required as part of the interview process to carve something out of a bar of soap. I had to do it but I don't recall exactly what I chose to carve. The purpose is to get an idea of an applicants dexterity.

After relying on this test for twenty-five years or so, the Department of Head and Neck Surgery at Kaiser Permanente Medical Center in Oakland, California, went back and looked at the original carvings of applicants and then at their skills in practice. I imagine there was some disappointment and even some chagrin in their report's final conclusion that, "Manual dexterity aptitude testing in the form of soap carving does not appear to correlate with surgical skill at the time of graduation."

Mothers of children born with facial disfigurements like missing ears, whether genetic or caused by other factors, often suffer terrible guilt. Sometimes they believe they caused it by having done something wrong during pregnancy. In some cultures there is a social stigma attached.

One mother in Bangladesh burst into tears of relief when I assured her, "It was not your fault your child had a deformity and the chance of your next baby having the same problem is very small." I always make a point of counseling and reassuring parents that their child's deformity occurred naturally.

There is no such thing as a routine medical mission. Although the doctors will often receive advance scans and other diagnostic information about specific patients they will be treating, what you find on arrival is often a crowd of anxious mothers who have traveled some distance hoping their child will be chosen. Nothing I had seen before, however, prepared me for a mission I participated in to Liberia.

It had been five years since the country's second civil war and what we found was the manifestation of an old Swahili proverb, Wapiganapo tembo nyasi huumia: When elephants fight it is the grass that suffers.

With two of my mentors, Dr. Moore and Dr. James Sidman, we traveled to the Bong County as part of the nonprofit group Children's Surgery International, based in Minnesota. We were to work out of Phebe Hospital, site of some of the worst atrocities committed during the war. As a child I had lived through a military coup but was never exposed to the violence and had never been in a war zone.

The main focus of our mission was to repair lip and palate defects. Before arriving we had posters distributed around the region showing before and after photos of cleft lips and palates, and announcements about the free surgeries were broadcast by radio. The response to free surgery in Africa is often overwhelming and there is always a crowd of mothers with children there to greet us. The reception in Liberia was all that and more.

Our van had just rolled into the hospital courtyard and our team members were assembling to take a ceremonial group photo when a nurse came running from the emergency room yelling for help. A child of about ten years had fallen from a tree and arrived at the hospital with a three-foot-long tree branch sticking out of both sides of his neck.

To the uninitiated, it seemed a miracle he was alive. Yet he was quite calm.

With no x-ray or scan to tell us exactly where the branch was, we rushed him to the operating room, sawed off one end of the stick and gently pulled the rest out the other side. He was one lucky little fellow because none of the vital blood vessels and nerves had been injured and he was able to leave the hospital the next day.

We did see a few deformities but more commonly we saw the effects of war. The first full day we screened more than two hundred children. By midday a disturbing pattern was emerging. There were a surprising number of children between five and seven with unrepaired lip and palate defects. These defects are usually repaired within the first year of life. We learned that the older children had been born during the peak of the civil war when mission groups like ours could not safely travel to Liberia.

Among the older children we saw, those between about ten and sixteen, there were missing ears or noses that had been hacked off with machetes. Like the boy with the stick through his neck, they were lucky to be alive, and those who found us were lucky to have the chance to have ears and noses rebuilt for them.

Those experiences haunt anyone who has ever participated in a mission to a former war zone. Sometimes I will lie in bed waiting for sleep and think about all those innocent children who could be helped were it available. My visit to Liberia was both exhilarating for what we had accomplished and disheartening. But it did prepare me for what I found when I travelled on a mission to Rwanda several years after the brutal genocide and machete hackings that took place there.

In my role as a facial reconstructive surgeon at Johns Hopkins Hospital in Baltimore, figuring out how to save or rebuild faces is complex but is the sort of surgery that is often planned well in advance. It requires the resources of a large teaching hospital like Hopkins, and the costs are typically paid for by insurance and other sources.

On the other hand, Hopkins is also an inner-city hospital where we see a number of patients who are "least among us" and who we treat for free. As a teaching professor with multiple responsibilities, it would be expedient for me to avoid these cases and let someone else handle them. But I can't.

Before I left Ghana to go to Russia, I had made that pact

with God—if my family could have a proper home again, I would devote my life to helping others. Keeping my end of the bargain was a solemn obligation—at home and abroad. So when a colleague at the hospital who takes on more than his share of these "least among us" cases asks for my help, I do my best to be available. "I have this patient," he'll say, "but he doesn't have insurance."

We work out the details between us and plan the surgery to use our time as efficiently as possible. One day he asked me to help with a patient from the homeless community who been diagnosed with cancer of the tongue. We needed to take out his tongue, after which I would try to fashion a useful tongue-like structure with tissue and nerves from other sites from his body.

Besides his tongue, his teeth were in such terrible condition he had packed his bleeding, weeping gums with bunched-up scraps of newspaper. As I pulled out the soaked wads it was hard to keep from gagging at the stench of rotting gum and diseased teeth.

Among the nurses, anesthesiologist, and other support staff there was a sudden outpouring of disgust.

"Oh, man, it smells so bad!"

"Yuck! How can anybody live like that?"

"Gross!"

This man, for whatever reason, did not have the choices the rest of us did. A pointed reminder was in order. I paused in my work and looked around the operating room to let everyone know I was addressing all of them.

"You see that he's homeless. Yes, his mouth is in awful shape. But the day he was born, somebody was very happy for him, and see where he is now. It can happen more easily than you know." Then I resumed unpacking his gums.

I didn't fault the people in that operating room for feeling disgust. My purpose was to remind them to count their blessings and retain their compassion so we could focus on doing our best for the patient, regardless of how repellent and inexplicable his condition might seem.

My point of view comes from my youthful experiences and also the international missions. Some of the like-minded doctors I've travelled with, who have become my friends, I met during my schooling and residency. Others I met while working on difficult cases or on the missions themselves.

All of my most cherished colleagues share a passion for the work and get their satisfaction from giving someone who wouldn't otherwise have it a chance to live a normal life or, in some cases, a life at all. For example, the operation to fix certain birth defects takes about an hour and in most cases is relatively straightforward. In places where medical missionaries go there are no surgeons to perform them.

At the other end of the spectrum, some cases I have worked on overseas have involved complicated disease-related deformities that would eventually have killed the patient at worst and, at best, left them with horrifying disfigurements and permanent alienation from their societies. One of these occurred in Rwanda involving a child of about eleven years old whose condition at first appeared to be uncomfortable and discomforting to look at but quickly turned into a life-or-death procedure.

This boy had a tumor growing in one of his nostrils. The people on the ground in Rwanda sent a CT scan and

I received a diagnosis on the nature of the growth. I wrote back, "We can take care of it." It was a straightforward procedure with little reconstructive surgery necessary. I didn't think twice about it.

We arrived in Rwanda within a week or so and got a chance to examine the boy. I was shocked to find that in such a short time the tumor had grown much bigger and was now protruding out of his nose. His case had become a little complicated, so we arranged to do the surgery in a private hospital where the equipment would be more sophisticated.

I saw the boy on a Sunday. Although it was clear he was in some pain, he made eye contact and was engaged when we asked him some basic questions. I told the team to schedule the surgery for three days later, on a Wednesday.

When I went to see the boy on Wednesday, I was stunned. In those few days the tumor had doubled in size. The boy was listless, lifeless—literally on death's doorstep. You could tell from his face that he had no strength left. A tumor as aggressive as that doesn't have to attack vital organs to kill. It does so by consuming all the energy the body needs to function. The tumor was rapidly dividing and growing its own network of blood vessels.

After an emergency transfusion, we changed the plan for how we were going to do the surgery and quickly got that tumor out. Within two hours, the procedure was successfully completed. When I went to see him in the recovery room he already looked better. By the end of the week, he was sitting up, eating, talking, back to being a normal kid with a nose that, when healed, would not look any different from any other kid's. That made the whole trip worthwhile.

Any doctor who has ever participated in such a mission has many stories to tell that are heart-breaking, uplifting, and sometimes just astonishing. A colleague, Dr. Ife (short for Ifeolumipo) O. Sofola, who also specializes in facial reconstructive surgery, tells the story of one of his most rewarding mission experiences. It is remarkable for how unremarkable the procedure was, yet how profoundly it changed the patient's life.

The mission was to a village in Nigeria, Dr. Sofola's native country. As usual, word quickly spread. On the first day a crowd had formed of mothers with children, doing their best to get attention.

"In the crowd," Dr. Sofola recalled, "was this young fellow, a seventeen-year-old boy, who was anxiously clamoring for attention but was incoherent. I couldn't make sense of anything he was trying to say.

"The older villagers, elbowing him aside, assured me that this young man was the village idiot. 'What is this guy saying?' I asked. 'Don't worry about him,' they said. 'He's just retarded.' But he was relentless.

"When I asked him his name, his response was unintelligible. But there was something about the look on his face and the sounds he was making that seemed inconsistent with mental impairment.

"'Open your mouth and stick your tongue out,' I ordered. He opened his mouth, but his tongue just quivered. 'Hold it right there.'

"I fetched a pair of hemostats (clamps used to prevent bleeding during surgery). I reached into his mouth, positioned the clamp, and grabbed the frenulum, a fold of skin beneath the tongue that you can see in the mirror when you curl it upward.

"I snipped, snipped, snipped. Then I asked him again, 'What's your name?'

"As clear as a church bell, he replied, 'My name is John.'

"Gasps of disbelief rose from the crowd and everyone stared at him and then at me with eyes as big as dinner plates. They'd just witnessed what was to them a miracle, pure and simple.

"It was a miracle, but not of a medical nature. It was a miracle—God's handiwork—that put me in that place at that moment with my diagnostic instincts at full power.

"'You mean he's not an idiot?' the villagers asked. I shook my head.

"In the five seconds it had taken me to cut this bit of skin that had restricted his tongue from moving since birth, a procedure that required zero stitches, he had been transformed from the least among them to an intelligent, articulate human being. He was suddenly a superstar.

"That boy followed me for the whole week we were there. Every time I turned around, there he was, his eyes flooding with gratitude. His diction was rusty and he asked me to cut some more, thinking that would help. 'Now it's up to you to go learn your diction,' I said. 'There's nothing else to cut.'"

One of my own favorite stories, although bittersweet, is about a mother in Bangladesh whose son had a cleft lip I repaired. It was a routine surgery and I came out of the operating room to meet with her. A translator explained that the operation had been a success and she could expect her child to live a normal life, news I love delivering.

But upon hearing it, the mother burst into tears that were clearly not joyful. I asked the translator to tell her, "No, this is good news! There were no complications and everything is going to be fine. Your son is perfect."

I was certain there had been a misunderstanding. But upon hearing the news a second time, her crying devolved into the most intense wailing, the sort associated with profound grief. Nothing we said would calm her. It was nearly a half hour before she had exhausted herself and could speak in between sobs.

As the translator listened his shoulders slumped. When the mother finished, he turned to me, his eyes shimmering.

"Dr. Boahene, it appears she had several children before this who were born with this condition and died as a result. She is grateful but she is mourning the babies she lost that could have been saved."

It was a humbling moment that moved me as well.

Dr. Sofola and I first met at a meeting of the American Academy of Facial Plastic and Reconstructive Surgery in Washington, DC. We spotted each other—one African recognizing another—across a large room full of doctors. It was, as he likes to put it, "love at first sight."

Dr. Sofola had been born in the US when his parents, college students from Nigeria, were completing their educations in Washington, DC. The family returned to Nigeria when he was an infant and that's where he grew up, returning to the States when he was seventeen. He earned a Bachelor of Science in biochemistry at the University of New Mexico. He studied medicine at Emory University School of Medicine in Atlanta, and did his training at Grady Hospital, the primary hospital serving Atlanta's indigent residents.

He went on to do his internship at Bethesda Naval Hospital in Maryland, the one where US presidents go when they need treatment. Then he went to flight school to learn how to fly jets and eventually became a naval flight surgeon, deployed on the aircraft carrier *USS Enterprise*.

After completing his tour of duty, he returned to Bethesda to do his residency in otolaryngology—head and neck surgery—now Dr. Top Gun and, according to his children, the coolest dad in the world.

It was during that time that we met. Ife was dressed in his brilliant white class A naval uniform, festooned with medals and ribbons. With his dark skin and pure white outfit, he cut quite an impressive figure. Even in a business suit, he would have stood out because twenty-five years ago there were just a handful of black doctors in our specialty and an even smaller number who were native Africans.

Like two powerful magnets, one look and we were walking briskly toward each another, smiling broadly and pushing chairs and tables out of the way in our haste.

Ife recalls, "I could identify from the immediate introduction that we had shared similar experiences and had the same aspirations. I could read the profound confidence in Kofi's eyes, and I'm sure he could see the same in mine. We were from the same sub-Saharan region of Africa. We were by definition brothers."

Our friendship was one of those rare relationships that seem to start off as though you've known each other all your lives. We are both Christians and our faith includes the conviction that God, not coincidence, brought us together, just as God sent Ife to Nigeria to make it possible for a tongue-tied boy to speak his first words.

Furthermore, although our profession is based in science, we both believe in the healing power of and faith. Ife once told me the story of his mother's death that illustrates our view that the true source of healing is in the unknowable.

Ife's mother was in the final stages of liver failure. He arranged for her to be brought to Bethesda Naval Hospital where she slipped into a coma with a Do Not Resuscitate order, reserved for patients who cannot be saved. Those three words mean that medicine has failed and loved ones must prepare for an imminent loss.

The family was heartbroken and his sister was persuaded by a friend to bring in a traditional tribal healer all the way from Africa. She kept it a secret until the Nigerian healer showed up in their mother's hospital room.

"I was dismayed," Ife told me, "and agitated by this man having been inserted into our family crisis. But there was nothing to lose so my siblings and I let him stay. The healer instructed us to hold hands in a circle around my mother's bed and pray.

"We had been praying in silence for only five minutes when the healer abruptly said, 'It is done,' and left to take a taxi back to the airport. It was a relief that he wasn't going to launch into some long-winded or undignified ceremony that might have upset the family.

"I thought, Well that's it, then. Twenty minutes later, my mother woke up, smiled, greeted us all, got out of bed, and took a shower. I was utterly dumbstruck. My heart was overflowing with joy and I dashed out into the hallway to announce, shouting, 'A miracle has occurred! Here, at Bethesda! A MIRACLE!'"

Ife's mother left the hospital and spent precious days with her children at home, saying goodbye. Her explanation for the sudden recovery was beautiful. "I came back so you would have faith." She died within a few weeks, having left a very big and lasting impression on everyone who knew her.

Ife said he thought about how many hours he'd spent in lecture halls, how many books he had studied, how many operations he had performed and concluded, "We are doctors so therefore we think we know something about life and death. In fact, I wonder sometimes if we know anything at all."

CHAPTER 19:
THE PRIMAL
FACIAL CASE

My friend Ife Sofola's comment about the limits of our knowledge as physicians about life and death speaks to the unique challenges that doctors sometimes face, even—and sometimes especially—within their own families. We know so much about the workings of the human body and all the things that can go wrong. In my case, this has been the cause of occasional anxiety.

When my wife, Adjoa, was a teenager she had a premonition that she would one day give birth to twins. It had always been in the back of her mind and when she learned she was pregnant, she just assumed it would be twins. In fact, the rate of twin births among Ghanaians (and throughout Central Africa) has statistically been the highest in the world—about three times the rate in the US, for example. The centre of this "twin zone" is Igbo-Ora, a small town in southwestern Nigeria. It is speculated by some researchers that besides genetics, a substance found in yam, a staple diet in West Africa, is partly responsible for the high twin rate.

Adjoa was so convinced she would have twins that when it turned out to be one child, a healthy girl we named Akuah, she was happy but surprised.

Two years later, in 2004, as I was starting my one-year fellowship in facial plastic and reconstructive surgery under Dr. Peter A. Hilger and Dr. James Sidman at the University of Minnesota, Adjoa became pregnant again. This time, she was even more convinced, and specific. "I'm sure I'm going to have twin boys this time." There was no earthly way for her to know. It was just a strong feeling she had—a premonition, a deeply felt wish, the guiding hand of God.

Soon after we moved to our new home in Edina, Minnesota, she flew home to New Zealand to help with a sister's wedding. Focused on the preparations, she wasn't paying much attention to the pregnancy except that she was having some discomfort.

One morning, soon after the wedding, she was feeling enough discomfort that she told her parents, a physician and a nurse. They immediately arranged for her to see an obstetrician. Her mother was with her when the technician performed the scan.

"Is this your first scan?" His eyes were fixed on the screen.

"Well, I had one in the States, but just for the heartbeat."

The ultrasonographer leaned toward the screen.

"Okay, so then we know about baby A and baby B?"

Adjoa started crying and then laughing and then crying some more. Her mother joined in. The racket must have been heard throughout the town. She immediately called me and I, too, burst into tears of joy. Ghanaians like to have large families. We felt so blessed to be having an extra child this time around, two boys!

As a physician and as a medical missionary I often work with sick children, and this is why I sometimes feel I know too much. When most children complain that their backs hurt, in the absence of an obvious answer most parents will assume something minor has happened. Perhaps they fell off their bikes and bruised themselves. They tend to shrug it off as normal childhood wear and tear.

When *my* children tell me their back hurts, I immediately begin the diagnostic process. Could it be a kidney tumor? A spine lesion? Since I became a husband and father, it has always been that way for me, mentally thumbing through the encyclopedia of dreadful diagnoses.

So I was especially alert the day I went with Adjoa to have a follow-up ultrasound after she returned from New Zealand. Every birth is slightly different, but with a mother carrying twins, there are more potential complications. When I can, I avoid mentioning my profession when I am a consumer rather than a provider. I don't want to intimidate any other medical professionals or somehow skew the care provided.

But I watched as intently as any doctor as the ultrasonographer glided the probe over Adjoa's belly. She paused in one spot and leaned closer to the screen.

"Oh, this looks good! The heartbeats are fine, and everything is fine." I exhaled with relief. "Oh," she added casually, "and the heads are together," and continued scanning.

I heard nothing she said after that. All I heard was a roaring in my ears: "the heads are together." When the technician was done, I nervously asked, "So, is everything okay?"

"Oh, I can't tell you anything like that. You have to talk to the obstetrician. He's the expert."

My brain became feverish with anxiety. Heads together? Conjoined twins? The complications from that sort of pregnancy are profound, life threatening, life changing. Visions of endless surgeries and a litany of nightmarish scenarios came rushing at me.

As calmly as I could manage, I asked the ultrasonographer, "Could you show me the heads again?"

She moved the sensor back across Adjoa's belly. "Okay, see this is Baby A and this is Baby B. Their heads are together."

They did appear to be touching. My stomach churned. Are they fused and the technician doesn't realize it?

"I want you to show it to me again. Move a little this way, please."

She gave me a peevish look, as if to say, What's up with this guy? Then I saw something that made my heart soar—a space. The boys were not conjoined. I said a silent prayer of thanks.

This experience, among others, has informed how I talk to my patients. I am very careful about how I explain things. I avoid technical medical terms. I often draw a picture to help the patient understand. The quiet terror I felt that day— which I did not share with Adjoa—showed me how different it is to be on the other side, as a patient or the parent of a child facing a potential health crisis.

Because my specialty deals with head and neck cancers, I often deliver bad news. It doesn't matter whether my patient is a billionaire prince or a homeless drug addict, when I have to say, "This is the cancer you have," they nearly always fall apart emotionally.

When the patient is a child, the crisis is multiplied. Parents will often give up lifelong careers to take care of a child with a debilitating disease. Everything I say to a patient and family is received as gospel, so I am always thinking about how it's going to be interpreted. Chief among the core commandments in the medical profession is to always leave people room for some hope, no matter how dismal we experts believe the prognosis to be.

When a doctor utters certain words to certain people, they often block out anything else, just as I did. An oncologist could tell a patient, "You have a brain tumor that experience and statistics tell us will kill you within a year." That's unambiguous but it leaves not a ray of hope.

Instead, a doctor is likely to tell a patient, "You have a brain tumor that is incurable, but we have a treatment protocol that 90 percent of patients tolerate very well." What he means is that the tumor is likely to cause death within a relatively short period of time, but there are therapies that have a good chance of buying them a little extra time and/or quality of life. And there are always experimental treatments that sometimes show promise. The door to hope is always open and there are many stories of patients who defied the odds to keep it open.

But the only words echoing in the heads of the patient and the family members may be "incurable" or may be "tolerate very well." Some will come away devastated, understanding there is no hope of returning to health and that a clock with an unknown amount of time on it has started counting down. Others will come away feeling hopeful and telling friends and family about that 90 percent figure.

These are things you can't teach a medical student. You can only know them by being on the other side.

One of the many things that makes my particular specialty unique and interesting is that we deal with the most intimate self-identity issue in the human psyche—what we see in the mirror and how other people react to our faces. During my residency and fellowship training, many medical students were overwhelmed at first by procedures that touch on such visceral feelings.

Once at the Mayo Clinic, we were performing a surgery around a patient's eye and needed the opinion of an ophthalmologist. When the consultant came to the operating room, he was followed by a medical student who was interested in pursuing ophthalmology as a specialty.

I took an instrument and retracted the eyelids apart, revealing the eyeball and the area of concern. Within seconds, the medical student turned pale and collapsed. We now had a second patient. The operating room nurse had seen this happen many times and knew exactly what to do. Our student blazed with embarrassment when she recovered. We reassured her this was not uncommon.

"Facial surgery is very different from doing abdominal surgery or heart surgery," my fellowship professor, Dr. Hilger, once explained. "A medical student who comes into our operating room to watch the removal of a gall bladder is only looking at the abdomen. Few of them go through the fainting stage when they first see someone being cut open."

He said medical students faint with much greater frequency when it's the face being operated on because, "You're connecting with the person who's having the surgery. The face is the person's identity and that has a much more profound emotional impact. Removing a gall bladder leaves a small scar in a spot most people never see.

"When it comes to the face, it isn't just about taking something apart—removing tissue and sewing the patient back up. When it comes to the face, you have to find ways to hide incisions and design surgeries that will reconstitute that which you took away, while avoiding damage to vital nerves and muscles that control facial expressions."

The Rwandan child who had the runaway tumor growing out of his nose is a good, if relatively simple, example. First we had to remove the tumor, making sure no cancerous tissue was left behind to grow another. Then we had to reform that section of his nose that had to be removed with the tumor so that, when he was healed, no one would ever know he'd had a problem.

Dr. Hilger recalls attending a talk by one of the doctors on the team that performed the first-ever partial face transplant, in Amiens, France, in 2005. There had been two cases of people having their own faces reattached after being torn off in accidents. In both cases, the detached tissue was rushed to the hospital where surgeons were able to reconnect the arteries and replant the skin.

The partial face transplant in France was on a woman who had been mauled by her dog. A section of face tissue from a woman who was brain-dead was grafted on to the patient's face. The French doctor said that when the swelling, bruising, and other visible effects of the surgery had resolved, the woman referred to the result as "the face," as though it were a mask, not part of her.

During the procedure, the surgeons were able to connect nerves not only for displays of emotion (smiling, frowning), but also for touch. Nerves take time to heal. Using periodic brain-imaging scans during her long recovery, the doctors could tell when she first started to perceive sensation by monitoring the areas in the brain that were active when her skin was stimulated by touch. What the doctors found most interesting was that as she began to be able to feel her new skin she stopped calling it "the face" and started calling it "my face."

Virtually every patient who has surgery on the face, whether it's reconstructive or cosmetic, experiences some degree of emotional stress. It begins with how they look immediately after surgery—swollen, bruised, bandaged. To some degree, all such patients have trouble connecting with the person they're seeing in the mirror, radically so with reconstructive surgery to correct wounds or remove tumors. Unlike the surgeon who removes your gall bladder or implants an artificial hip, facial surgeons have a responsibility to determine whether a patient is psychologically suited, make sure they understand the process, and help them through the transition after surgery until they are at home with the new look.

Dr. Hilger once told me, "A person may be the world's most outstanding surgical technician, but he stinks if he doesn't have the people skills to help his patients through this process." Those skills include discouraging some people who may have body dysmorphic disorder (BDD)—an obsession with some minor aspect of their person they feel is so flawed it prevents them from leading a normal life.

Someone with BDD might say, "I can't go out in public because I have this huge bump on my nose," and it really isn't much of a bump. Or, "I have these terrible asymmetries and I can't go out in public because I know people are staring at me," when in fact the person may be fundamentally attractive. BDD is a psychiatric disorder and those who suffer from it can become just as reclusive as someone with a truly deformed face.

I once heard of a patient who believed he had huge hump on his nose and wanted it removed. Nasal hump reduction is a common procedure and usually ends with a good result and satisfied patient. This particular patient apparently had BDD but had hidden the signs well enough to convince the plastic surgeon to remove the hump. With the hump reduced, his body dysmorphism became fully manifest. He felt so incomplete that he cut a piece off a toothbrush handle and taped it to his nose where the hump had been.

In America and in other developed nations, the term plastic surgery is synonymous with narcissism. To most Americans, a plastic facial surgeon does eye lifts and face lifts, fixes noses, inserts chin enhancements, and injects Botox—procedures that patients think will make them look younger or more attractive.

As an African facial surgeon, I am often challenged by patients to explain why, with all the poverty and disease in

Africa, I would choose a specialty that glamorizes aesthetic appearance and caters to the rich and famous. Considering where I started out and what it took for me to get to where I am, and considering how much time I have devoted to medical missions, I should be insulted.

Instead I explain that modern plastic surgery as a specialty was an outcome of war. The father of modern plastic surgery is generally considered to have been Sir Harold Gillies of New Zealand who, like myself, was an otolaryngologist. Working in London during the First World War, he developed many of the techniques of modern facial surgery while caring for soldiers who had suffered all sorts of disfiguring facial injuries from shrapnel, bullets, and chlorine gas.

That is the tradition I have followed. Instead of soldiers, the enemy today is often a cancer of the head and neck that, when removed, leaves a patient with devastating disfigurements. The treatment for some cancers requires removing the lower jaw, or the tongue, or a large section of the face. Such heroic surgeries can offer a new lease on life or at least an extension. But what patients worry about most is, "How am I going to look? I just don't want to scare my grandchildren." These are not narcissistic questions. They are fundamental to a person's mental health.

The late Francis Cooke Macgregor, a renowned social scientist and a pioneer researcher in the field of facial deformities and plastic surgery, once described facial disfigurement as a "psychological and social death." She was the first scholar to document the suffering of facial disfigurement through birth, accident, disease, or war. She was also a photographer whose interest in our self-image was sparked while taking pictures of patients at a cancer hospital in Columbia, Missouri.

She later met plastic surgeon Dr. John Marquis Converse, who specialized in repairing the shattered and burned faces of French and English pilots during World War II. They ended up collaborating on the first major study of the psychosocial problems associated with even minor cosmetic surgery.

After interviewing and tracking hundreds of patients and their families, she wrote three books that are known as Macgregor's Trilogy: *Facial Deformities and Plastic Surgery*, *Transformation and Identity*, and *After Plastic Surgery*. Before she died at the age of ninety-five in 2001, Macgregor and other researchers were estimating that as many as one in ten people in the developed world had a disfigurement—a scar, blemish, or deformity—which seriously hindered their capacity to lead a normal life.

Although I do perform cosmetic surgeries as part of my practice, the work that gives me the greatest satisfaction is using my skills to remove tumors or repair a malformation and put that person back together in such a way that they can go out in public without fear of being stared at or ridiculed. Like Dr. Hilger, I am dismayed by the psychological effect on people who live in a culture obsessed with physical perfection when there are so many people around the world whose very life depends on such simple things as an intact upper lip.

What I am most proud of are some of the innovative procedures I have been able to pioneer and others I have refined that go beyond the face and inside the cranium. These often involve removing tumors and fixing other medical conditions that would otherwise lead to blindness or an early death.

It is very fulfilling when I can rewire a face that has lost the ability to smile or restore facial expression in a child born with undeveloped facial nerves. When patients thank me for my efforts, I tell them, "Pay me with a smile." For these highly complex procedures, I keep on my desk a skull that I often pick up and contemplate, much like Hamlet. In my case, however, I am not brooding about death but about how to preserve and enhance life.

CHAPTER 20: COMING TO HOPKINS

When Adjoa called from New Zealand to tell me that we were expecting twins, my first thought after getting over the initial shock was that I now needed a "real" job. Five years of residency training had all the elements of a real job—long hours, stress, and a stipend. But it felt more like on-the-job training.

Like my father, I felt responsible for taking care of not only my immediate family but also—like many immigrants from less-developed countries—my family back home in Ghana. I received offers to join private practice groups performing cosmetics surgery, which would have been financially rewarding. Because of my dual training in otolaryngology as well as plastic surgery, my options were broader than that.

What appealed to me most, but would be less remunerative, was academic medicine. I wanted to be able to teach and mentor future doctors while exploring surgical frontiers so

I limited my job search to academic hospitals. My hard-won Mayo pedigree and having trained with my noted fellowship mentors Drs. Hilger and Sidman made me an attractive candidate.

I wrote to the chairs of otolaryngology departments at nearly two dozen leading medical centers around the country. I described my background, training, vision, and the contribution I hoped to make if offered a position. Six of them responded and interviews were arranged. In December 2004, I was thrilled to receive an offer from the Johns Hopkins University Hospital in Baltimore, consistently ranked as one of the top institutions in the world and, at that time, ranked number one among US medical institutions.

Like the Mayo Clinic and Meharry Medical College, Hopkins has a storied and inspiring history that combines elements of the other two. The original money, land, and mission were provided in the will of Johns Hopkins, a successful Baltimore merchant and banker who died in 1873. Hopkins had been a Quaker, a religious sect that advocated non-violence and the abolition of slavery. Fifty-five years before the Civil War and the Emancipation Proclamation, when Johns Hopkins was twelve years old, his family was among the first plantation owners south of the Mason-Dixon line to free their slaves. Hopkins had gone into business with three of his brothers selling wares from wagons. Most of his wealth came later from investments in railroads.

In his will he directed that two institutions be built: Johns Hopkins University and The Johns Hopkins Hospital that would provide the best care by physicians and surgeons "of the highest character and greatest skill." He also left money to build an orphanage for black children. At the time, his was the largest philanthropic bequest in US history.

Hopkins's vision was revolutionary—two institutions in which medical practice, research, and education would be integrated under one roof. The Mayos had set the stage for group medical practices. Hopkins is credited with providing the money and vision for the first teaching hospital.

Hopkins appealed to me because of this rich history and its focus on and leadership in surgical innovation.

One of the most remarkable stories I had read about medical discoveries was the partnership between Alfred Blalock, a pioneering Johns Hopkins heart surgeon, and Vivien Thomas, an African American surgical laboratory assistant. Their collaboration resulted in the development of life-saving surgery for "blue baby" syndrome. Blue babies are those born with a defect in the development of the heart chambers called Tetralogy of Fallot (named for a French physician). The malformation allows blood from the heart to bypass the lungs. As a result, inadequately oxygenated blood is recirculated causing the infant's skin to turn blue and leading to death.

Vivien Thomas's story is one of the most extraordinary in medical history. He was born in Louisiana, the grandson of a slave, and went to high school in Nashville, Tennessee, the home of my alma mater, Meharry Medical College. After high school he got a job as a carpenter's apprentice at Vanderbilt University, saving his money for college, after which he intended to go to medical school.

After the stock market crash of 1929, he was laid off from his carpentry job but through a friend found work as a research assistant in the animal laboratory of Dr. Alfred Blalock, a young surgeon at Vanderbilt Hospital who had earned his medical degree at Johns Hopkins. Thomas had a gift for the work and a brilliant mind for research, and the two men became a team. In 1940, when Dr. Blalock was hired by Johns Hopkins hospital as chief of surgery, he convinced Thomas to go with him and run the hospital's surgical research laboratory. The only other black employees at the hospital then were janitors.

Their partnership resulted in several groundbreaking discoveries, including the design of an innovative surgical technique for treating infants born with blue baby syndrome. Standing on a stool beside Dr. Blalock in the operating room, Thomas—who had invented some of the tools for this procedure and had performed it in dogs—talked through the steps as Dr. Blalock performed the pioneering surgery on babies. Although Thomas never earned a degree himself, his collaboration with Blalock saved thousands of children born with this defect and, by the end of his career, he was regarded as a skilled surgeon and surgical instructor.

Like Vivien Thomas, my surgical career begun in an animal lab, in a veterinary hospital in Moscow. His experience—about breaking down racial barriers—made Hopkins that much more attractive.

When I first interviewed at Hopkins, I met Dr. Patrick J. Byrne, whose specialty was the same as mine and who had also completed his fellowship training with Dr. Hilger, my mentor. We shared a vision to make the division of facial plastic surgery one of the best in the country. I became the first recruit of Dr. Lloyd Minor, who had recently become chair of the department of otolaryngology, the first of its kind in the nation.

Dr. Minor's only concern was to make sure I would stick around. A number of people in my field who had been recruited to Hopkins left after a year or two for academic careers elsewhere or to go into private practice. One of the factors may have been Baltimore's reputation for being crime-riddled. At the time it was the setting for a wildly popular television series about inner-city crime called *The Wire*. I imagine candidates who were considering applying to Hopkins might have gotten looks of disbelief from colleagues just by mentioning it.

After I assured him I was prepared to make a long-term commitment and explained my life goals—to serve the least among us, bring better care to many, and inspire future generations of African health professionals—Dr. Minor invited me back for a second interview.

"And this time," he suggested, "why don't you come with your wife?"

It sounded like more than a casual suggestion but I thought it might have something to do with making sure my family would be comfortable with the commitment. As to Baltimore's reputation, I'd been in many places that could be considered much worse. So had my good friend Dr. Ife Sofola, who had done his internship at a similar inner-city hospital— Grady in Atlanta—and expressed no particular anxiety about his or his family's safety.

Adjoa had grown up in the peaceful cities of Wellington and Auckland, New Zealand, spent a year living in London, and had done a good bit of traveling around the world. But since marrying, we lived mostly in the small all-American town of Rochester, Minnesota, home to the Mayo Clinic.

Rochester is a quiet, prosperous Midwestern city of just over 100,000 about ninety miles south of Minneapolis. The crime rate there is about half the national average. The rate in Baltimore was seven times that, including hundreds of murders every year, earning it the unfortunate nickname Bodymore.

None of this crossed my mind when Adjoa and I flew to Baltimore for my second interview. The route from the airport to the Hopkins campus downtown takes you by necessity through local streets. Once we left the highway and began our approach, Adjoa stared out the window in silent dismay as we passed block after block of treeless, run-down neighborhoods of plain, two-story row houses, many of them boarded up or bearing the scorch marks of fire.

On a school day, young children loitered on front steps, the faces of vigilant mothers and older siblings watching from windows. On corners, clutches of menacing-looking men and boys loitered, eyeing us with challenging looks as we drove past.

Finally Adjoa blurted, "There's no way we are coming here!"

That evening Dr. Minor and his wife invited us to their suburban home. The Minors reassured Adjoa that employees of the hospital were well protected and that there were many safe neighborhoods to live in nearby. She relented and I arrived at Hopkins in July 2005 just as I got the news that I had won the Anderson Award for attaining the highest score in the entire nation on the Facial Plastic Surgery Board examination.

Two months before moving to Maryland, the twins—Baby A and Baby B—decided they were ready for their debut. The morning of their delivery I was called in for an emergency surgery at the Regions Hospital in St. Paul. A young man had been in a car accident and his larynx was crushed. A tracheotomy allowed him to breathe but the surgery to rebuild his windpipe and larynx couldn't be delayed.

I had nearly missed the delivery of Akua, our first child, and was praying to be able to be there this time. I made it, just in time to witness the safe delivery of our sons James and Jonathan and to welcome them into our family.

My first year in practice at Hopkins flew past. I was building a clinical practice while developing a niche in research. Each week I made a point of visiting physicians in the community to introduce myself. Most were welcoming but a few were quite rude. One practitioner told me, "I see you have had excellent training, but I will never refer patients to you." I had no idea how to respond so I thanked him for his time and quietly left his office. Fortunately the majority of my experiences were positive and the environment at Hopkins lived up to my early expectations.

It was amazing to be in a place where there was a leading expert in any field who could help me explore and develop any idea that might pop up into my mind. Tissue engineering researchers collaborated with me in rebuilding faces damaged by cancer and birth defects.

Sometimes when I'm in my office I will look out the window in wonder at the original cylindrical Hopkins hospital building (which gave us the medical expression "making the rounds"). I am reminded of the many times I almost gave up my quest or it was in danger of being denied me. I say a silent prayer of thanks for the faith, friendships, and random Samaritans without whom none of it would have been possible. Then I turn back to my desk where my Hamlet skull sits, waiting to provide me with solutions to problems I have yet to encounter.

CHAPTER 21: TIGHT SPOTS

I'd like to believe that, had I been born and raised in the US with all of its opportunities, I would still be doing the kinds of intricate, leading-edge surgeries that have saved lives and preserved or restored the dignity of many patients. Growing up in Ghana has been a great blessing and I wouldn't trade it for all the advantages in the world. Like the stream that never forgets its source, my cultural experiences have been and continue to be a constant source of inspiration.

For example, those toys I learned to make out of discarded cans and bits of wire and plastic gave me a unique set of creative tools. Inventing your own toys was good training for inventing less invasive and safer ways to treat diseases of the head and neck.

My colleagues who are neurosurgeons, who treat diseases of the brain, begin most of their procedures by cutting open the skull from the top to access the affected region. Instrument miniaturization, tiny cameras, and high-definition scans have made neurosurgery safer, less intrusive, and more effective than ever. But it still starts with a drill and saw.

When a neurosurgeon removes a brain tumor today, the patient is typically left with a scalp scar, but his or her face is intact. On patients with dense or long hair, you almost can't see the scar. Put on a hat and most people would never know.

In my specialty as an otolaryngology/head and neck surgeon, my most challenging work takes place beneath the brain, in the area called the skull base—behind the eyes and between the ears. To reach a tumor in this area can be very tricky and involve disassembling parts of the face—bone and connective tissue. This type of surgery used to require making an opening in the skull, which is harder on the patient, especially when the problem is below the brain.

Today we increasingly use a minimally invasive endo-scopic procedure in which instruments attached to a tiny camera lens are inserted through natural openings—the nose, mouth, a small hole just above the eyebrow, or by going in through a corner of the eye socket. The goal is to do as little damage as possible to the person's appearance while getting to the site and removing the diseased tissue. My Hopkins neurosurgery colleague, Dr. Alfredo Quinones-Hinojosa, and I have performed these procedures hundreds of times to remove tumors and repair brain fluid leaks.

What we have gained by not having to work around the brain is offset somewhat by skull base surgery's unique risks. These procedures often get close to the brain stem and spinal cord. It's quite a challenge to remove a tumor that is growing near or around that part of the head without causing more problems than you set out to solve. All of your cranial nerves are there—nerves that control motor skills, feeling, and taste, as well as the major arteries and veins that nourish the brain. We want to avoid compromising those functions by causing collateral damage.

Then there is the complex network of nerves around the face that, if injured, can cause facial paralysis. The patient may end up with a stroke-like affect—one side of the face is droopy and unresponsive. This can be a great loss—the ability to communicate emotions like happiness, especially when the patient is a child. Finally, facial surgeries can leave scars and distortions, some of which will heal or can be cosmetically repaired, but not always.

This surgical Times Square is my sweet spot. The procedures I do in the skull base usually begin with removing benign or cancerous growths and abnormalities on the underside of the brain and the first few vertebrae. Step two is reconstructing the face—replacing or substituting lost tissue and bone, repurposing healthy tissue, rewiring nerves, and so on. The final step is closing the surgical sites with very fine sutures and other methods that will leave the least scarring, and tucking them into wrinkles and creases where they will be least noticed. You can see now how it's kind of like inventing a toy car!

A neurosurgeon, on the other hand, can enter the brain without disturbing a person's face and focus solely on meticulous tumor removal. When his or her job is done, other doctors can step in to put the patient back together again using fairly standard techniques.

For me, the final step is often the greatest challenge,

so I begin thinking about a case by working from the end backwards. A successful end leaves the patient with a face that's as intact as possible. When I plan it out, I'm drawing on instincts learned from building my own toys, and on my experiences in places where we sometimes had to improvise.

On one medical mission, we were performing a surgery to screw a bone graft into a patient's jawbone when the medical drill we were using broke. The only alternative was to send someone to get a Black & Decker construction drill, put it inside a sterile bag, and finish the surgery.

On the other hand, my missionary experiences came into play at Johns Hopkins when I treated a woman in her mid-forties with a large skull base tumor. I was able to remove it by going in through her nose. When she was recovering, I explained that the tumor was in a confined space.

"In about six weeks we will get an MRI scan to make sure that nothing was missed. If there is anything, we will do what we call a second look—go back and take out whatever remained."

She came in for the MRI images and was with her family in the waiting room while I reviewed the scans. The images popped open on the screen and what I saw made my stomach flutter. There was a large tumor in the same area. It was the same size as the one I removed. For a second I thought the lab had given me the original MRI, from before the operation. Then I thought, Did I not see this tumor? Could I really have left this mass behind? Or did it grow back that quickly?

The pathology report indicated a non-aggressive cell type. If I had left some of it behind, which is not unusual in tight spots like that, it should not have grown so quickly. However, there are theories—yet to be confirmed by science—that when you disturb a tumor you can stimulate its growth.

I concluded that I probably left a bit of tumor because it was in an area that I knew I did not go into the first time. It was a disappointing shock, considering it had taken six hours of surgery to take out the original.

I knew that the patient and her family were eager to hear the news, but I needed a bit more time to process what had happened and think about the next step. So I popped my head into the cubicle in the waiting hall where they were gathered. Every head snapped to attention, searching my face for a clue. Sounding as confident and positive as I could, I said, "I'm having a problem pulling one particular image up, but I have not forgotten about you."

Those moments when I first enter the waiting room are often dramatic for me as well as the family. As soon as people see me coming, brows crease and hands are wrung. Everybody is on edge. Even when people know the person in the lab coat isn't their surgeon, the assumption is that he or she is coming to deliver important news.

It's a peculiar interaction and I've experienced it from both sides. I've had to take my father in for a surgery and even though it was routine and low-risk, I felt that same rush of adrenaline when the surgeon showed up to report the results.

When I'm able to deliver good news, which is often, it's the highlight of any day and I wear a relaxed smile that seems to calm everyone before I've uttered the first word. I may have been in surgery for twelve hours and it's midnight, but I always will take time to personally report to the family.

In this case, I needed a few extra minutes of close examination of the original scan and the new one to confirm that what I was seeing was a recent growth. I was disheartened to see that it was in a more difficult position to access than the original. When I returned to the family and explained the situation, everyone began crying. It was a difficult moment because I hadn't had time to think about the solution. I did my best to reassure them.

"We're in this together. I'm going to take care of it. You're going to be fine. I'm going to have to think about how to do it, but we'll take it out."

What I did not tell them was that the new tumor was in such a location that one of the treatment options might be to temporarily remove her jawbone, among other complications, and then put her back together once the tumor had been removed. That would be a very long operation with many surgical steps. The temporary disfigurement, the extensive facial reconstructive surgery that would be required, and a long recovery would have made for an extremely stressful experience and increased potential for complications.

Back at my desk, I picked up my Hamlet skull and turned it this way and that, poking a pen through this opening and that. Then the solution popped into my head, so instinctively that I chuckled aloud. Of course!

In Africa and elsewhere, my medical missions have included many cleft lip and palate repairs. A cleft lip contains an opening in the upper lip that may extend into the nose. A cleft palate is when the roof of the mouth contains an opening into the nose. The palate—the roof of your mouth—is located behind the nose and under the sinus cavities.

I was certain I could reach the tumor by creating a cleft

palate and then closing it back up when I was done. This made a complicated surgery simpler, although the tumor removal would still be a painstaking process. The surgery went well and two days later, once again tumor free, the patient went home with a sore mouth but with her face intact. That was a red-letter day.

In the early years of my career it was not uncommon for patients to cancel appointments when they found out that their specialist was black or from Africa, or just had a weird tongue-twister of a name. This came from both white and black patients, except one elderly African American man who, startled upon meeting me for his first appointment, declared, "If they let you in here, you must be good!"

Prejudice, expressed and acted out, was familiar to me after so many years, first in Russia and then in the US. I had learned to shrug it off. Besides the color of my skin, I have always looked a bit younger than my years so that was another liability at times. When these situations would arise, I'd remember my father's wisdom—a good name is better than riches. If I worked hard and took good care of people, I believed the good name would follow, and it has.

Coming up with innovative surgical solutions has earned me a reputation for being able to get to tumors in very hard-to-reach areas in the skull. I have been invited to present my techniques at international conferences and often been singled out for recognition. As a result, people who have heard or read about me now seek me out for consultations.

Each night when I get home, I often tell my wife, Adjoa, if it was a good or stressful day, but not much more than that. She once told me she used to wonder how much the bad days affected my emotional state because I tend not to talk about them much. It's not that I don't experience stress and anxiety, but I try to keep things in perspective and trust that certain outcomes might not be part of my plan but they are part of God's.

And then there are the evenings when I get home and tell her, "It was a REALLY stressful day." That's usually when I have a patient who has reached the end of his or her options and I've had to deliver the news to them and their loved ones, knowing it is probably the last time I'll ever see them. It may be someone who I've been treating for a long time and we've developed a rapport. It's not in my nature to accept easily that I can't invent my way out of every problem.

After days like that, I don't complain but I do become a bit less sociable and much more contemplative. I pray every day for every person I treat and if it's a tough situation, I will also ask God to give me the wisdom to do and say the right things. I try not to become too emotional but I occasionally get teary-eyed. So far, I've only broken down in front of a patient once, when surgery did not go the way I wanted. The patient survived but the disappointment I felt was overwhelming.

She was a young girl born with a vascular tumor filling her nose and upper jaw bones, severely deforming her face. The tumor had been successfully removed before she was five years old but her face failed to develop as she grew. She had no upper teeth, her face and nose were flat, and she had so much trouble breathing that when she went to bed at night she needed a machine to keep from suffocating. She was a sweet child and after a series of surgeries over seven years she had become a beautiful girl who was about to go off to college. There was one last thing she wanted—permanent teeth instead of the dentures she had to wear.

Using a computer, we were able to generate a precise model of her face and perform the surgery virtually before going into the actual operating room. All the planning paid off.

The surgery to do that required moving bone, adding bone that had been harvested from one of her legs, and other procedures. That was the most difficult part of the surgical plan and the result looked great. The next step, before closing her up, was to connect two blood vessels to supply the bone transplant with nourishment and oxygen. That procedure took about a half hour.

But when the vessels were connected, the blood wouldn't flow. I took everything out, did it again, but the blood supply still wouldn't go through. I turned to the anesthesiologist. "Is everything okay? What's the blood pressure?"

"She is not doing well," he said. "The blood-oxygen level is coming down and pressure is dropping. Something's not right."

Now this elegant surgery that was going to provide this young woman with the confidence to go out into the world and lead a full life had turned into a dire emergency. To keep trying to connect the vessels was too risky now that her vitals were deteriorating. We suspected that her blood was forming clots that were blocking her oxygenation. We had to stop, sew her up, and get her off the operating table as quickly as possible.

Eventually she was stabilized and we were able to send her to the Intensive Care Unit to recover. I was crushed. For seven years I had been working on that girl's face. I knew it as intimately as I'd known any patient's face. She was delightful and likable. I had watched her grow up and had an emotional investment in the outcome.

It would have been technically possible to try again, but the clotting made it too great a risk. The harvested bone could not be saved so we would have to harvest bone from her other leg, which I didn't want to put her through. I would have to tell her and her family, "We have to probably just give up this particular thing."

My heart ached as I entered the ICU where she was recovering, with everyone in her family looking to me for signs of hope. I opened my mouth to speak but my throat swelled shut and nothing would come out. My eyes flooded and tears streamed down my cheeks.

I had so very much wanted this to work for her, the final leg of her long, difficult journey. Technically, it was something I should have been able to give her. But every person's body is different. Unpredictable and inexplicable things happen. Sometimes you just reach the limits of what medicine can accomplish.

What made me feel even worse than having failed was that her family, seeing my distress, turned their attention to comforting *me*. "We know you did everything you could. You've taken such good care of her. It's okay."

As my friend Ife Sofola said when his dying mother seemed to spontaneously recover, we doctors think we know so much and we can do anything—until we come face to face with experiences that remind us that the hand of God is always at work behind the scenes.

CHAPTER 22:
FACE TO FACE

One of my patients, an African American woman, was vacationing with her daughter in Paris, out for a stroll, when she noticed coming the other way an elderly man with an intriguing face. As they passed, he glanced at her with smiling eyes. She felt a jolt of familiarity and stopped short.

"There's something about that man," she said to her daughter. "I think I want to sit and talk with him a bit."

"Mom, you can't just go talk to a stranger in Paris. For one thing, you don't speak any French."

"Well *you* do, so come on! I think I'd like to just talk with him for a minute."

They caught up with the stranger and invited him to have a coffee with them.

"Mais oui, ma fille!" Of course, daughter!

It was a greeting you might hear in certain parts of the world where an unrelated adult male is addressed by a child as uncle, or an older man might address a young woman he doesn't know as daughter—an expression of respect.

When they were settled in a cafe, the man said that when they'd passed each other he too had a feeling of familiarity. He had thought about turning around and coming back to talk to her because, "I know you are from my country."

"Oh? Which country is that?"

"Senegal."

It happened that this woman had recently gone through the process of having her DNA tested and matched with the region in Africa where her ancestors had come from. He was right—Senegal!

She was amazed. How many generations of her family had come and gone since they were enslaved and sent out of Africa hundreds of years ago? How many different races made up who she was—African, European, Native American? Yet she retained features that a modern-day Senegalese could spot in the split second of a glance. Even more amazing to her was the realization that somewhere in her primal subconscious was enough information to allow her to recognize him as a member of her tribe.

As a surgeon who has devoted his professional life to studying and treating the human face, I'm constantly reminded of the profound influence that appearance has on the quality and meaning of our lives. It's about much more than what we speak of as beauty or physical perfection. These are words whose meanings change according to the fads and fashion of the time.

The central role that the face plays in shaping lives is reflected in the hundreds of sayings, proverbs, and expressions that refer to it. When we embarrass ourselves we lose face. When we accept the inevitable, we face the music. In confronting competitors we may face them down or have a face off. When we decide to meet in person instead of talking on the phone we meet face to face. We may reconsider a proposal when someone puts a new face on it. Entire books have been written about how to read another person's mood by paying attention to the shape and position of the mouth, eyes, and forehead.

Recognition software has established that no two faces are exactly the same, even between identical twins. And as my patient learned from a random encounter on a Paris street, every face has a story to tell, even though the person behind the face may not know it.

The nineteenth-century American writer and philosopher Ralph Waldo Emerson once wrote, "A man finds room in the few square inches of his face for the traits of all his ancestors; for the expression of all his history, and his wants." That intense awareness of individual, racial, and cultural subtleties and what they mean to people when they see themselves in the mirror or in the reactions of others helps inform my approach to every surgery.

One of the conditions I have studied in detail is damage to the nerves that control the face. A person who is unable to display what they feel, or to tell a story, or whose face tells a misleading story because of a deformity or disease usually experiences isolation and often frustration in social situations.

My first big breakthrough occurred in 2008. It involved a child and it began by happenstance. A pediatrician was treating a one-year-old boy for a routine problem when he noticed the boy's three-year-old brother, who was along for the ride, had a smile that was slightly askew. The parents seemed unconcerned but the doctor's instincts told him a scan was in order.

His conscientiousness was rewarded when the scan revealed a tumor in the child's skull base that was impinging on a facial nerve. The tumor was benign, so it was possible that by doing nothing the boy would be okay, although his smile would remain slightly crooked. If the tumor continued to grow, however, it would eventually destroy the nerve and his face would be paralyzed. Removing the mass would involve severing the nerve.

A facial nerve does two things. It gives the facial muscles what we call tone, which is the ability to hold muscle and other tissues in place. Facial nerves also control movement. When a facial nerve is damaged or severed, the facial muscle loses its tone and becomes flaccid and sags. Left untreated for a year or two, the muscle withers away, resulting in permanent disfigurement and loss of the ability to display emotion.

In consulting with the surgeon who was going to remove the tumor, I discussed two scenarios.

"I can rewire the facial nerve first, to bypass the tumor so you don't have to worry about it during your procedure. Or, you can go ahead with the surgery and after you've removed the tumor, if it's possible to leave both ends of the severed nerve accessible, I can repair the gap by transferring nerve tissue from elsewhere."

At the time, nerve transplant and transfer surgeries were beginning to offer hope to patients whose extremities had been paralyzed or damaged in accidents. Moving nerves is common surgery in children who are born with a brachial plexus injury, which can occur during a breech birth. When force is required to extract the baby from the womb, the nerves from the neck going to the arm can tear, causing weakness or paralysis. The repair involves moving nerves from a muscle that is not so vital to one that is, like an arm or a hand that needs to be able to grip things.

In this case, we decided to go ahead with the surgery, remove the tumor and fix the nerve gap that would result. But when the tumor was removed, the portion of the nerve coming from the brainstem was completely gone. It would not be possible to bridge the gap.

I had already thought about that possibility, and how I might connect the loose end of the nerve where it connected to the facial muscles to a different nerve. For example, there is a muscle that allows us to chew that can be connected to a severed facial nerve in such a way that clenching your teeth produces a smile. It is like wiring a light switch except nerves take a long time to grow.

In this case I decided to connect the remaining portion of the boy's facial nerve to a nerve that controls his tongue. If it worked, which we wouldn't know for sure for months, his face would regain its tone and when the boy moved his tongue his face would respond. He would have to be taught how to use his tongue in this new way, but once he did learn it would be a matter of practicing until the sensors in his brain had gotten used to the new pattern. Because he was young, he was expected to adapt quickly. We would have to wait for signs that the connection of the two nerves was successful.

About three months after the surgery, I woke up very early one day and was checking my email when I spotted one from the address of the boy's father. It had been sent in the middle of the night, suggesting a crisis. I opened it bracing for bad news. "Dear Dr. Boahene," it began. "Tonight, for the first time in my son's life, I really saw him smile."

It was an emotional moment for me, also a father. I had no trouble imagining how he felt. That surgery became one of my most compelling success stories. If you saw that boy today you'd never suspect he ever had any problems.

There is a coda to this story that makes it even sweeter. The boy's grateful dad was intrigued and looked me up on the Internet. He found an interview in which I mentioned Jerry Manion, my organic spectroscopy professor at University of Central Arkansas who cosigned my school loans so that I could go to Meharry Medical College. The father tracked down Jerry's email address and wrote him a note with a picture of his smiling son attached to thank him for helping me and let him know the good that had come of it.

After that I started getting similar cases of faces that didn't look too bad but because of a tumor were destined to get worse. The procedure and the strategy has been and continues to be refined. When possible, I rewire the facial nerve before a tumor surgery and let it grow in. That way, when the tumor surgery is done the face is already working as it should and, in some cases, better than before.

Most people are familiar with Bell's palsy, the sudden onset of facial droop that is commonly confused for a stroke. Bell's palsy results from a viral inflammation of the facial nerve and resolves with little trace 90 percent of the time. For the unlucky ones the affected face either remains droopy or the opposite happens and the face becomes extremely taut.

The psychological effects of these sorts of conditions is

profound and transcends the social strata. One CEO of a major firm told me that he always eats well before going to company parties so he won't be hungry and have to run the risk of food dribbling out of his paralyzed lips. A woman said her grandchild avoids her because she is unable to form a smile and thus looks angry all the time. Many young women have told me tearfully that their inability to smile has robbed them of affection. These stories motivate me to find solutions.

Some children are born without the ability to smile. Their faces are in a perpetual frown and cannot reflect the joyful feelings kids often have inside. This disease is called Moebius syndrome. The nerves or muscles that normally move the face do not properly develop.

Each year I travel to Peru to work with local surgeons helping restore smiles to children born this way. During one such visit I asked a group of about fifteen children with Moebius syndrome to assemble for a photo. As I reflexively do when taking photos of my own kids, I asked them to smile for the camera, forgetting for a moment that they could not.

What happened next was emotionally overwhelming. In the last row a chubby, boisterous nine-year-old put his fingers in his mouth and pulled the corners to simulate a

smile. He did this so naturally and flawlessly it was clear he had done it a million times. His face glowed with innocent childish mirth. In that instant he stole my heart. I vowed to give him a real smile, which we did.

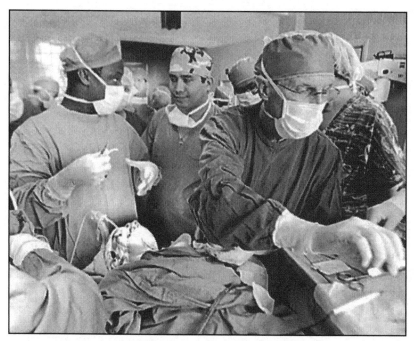

The scene in the operating room in Peru as we prepare to reconstruct the face of a young child. To my immediate left is Dr. Juan Francisco Ore, a Peruvian maxillofacial surgeon. My mentor, Dr. Peter Hilger, is on the right.

A Peruvian boy after successful surgery to give him a real smile.

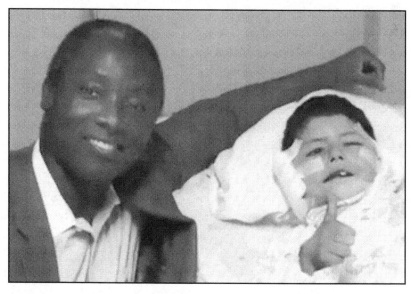

At times, patients defy the odds and teach us a lesson. Anna was a six-year-old from a small town in Germany who was born with Moebius syndrome. Her dream was to be able to smile before starting her school years.

I saw her on one of my trips to Germany as a visiting professor. Anna and her parents spoke only German, challenging me to reach back into my memory for the German I learned in Ghana when I thought I would be attending a German medical school.

They told me that playing with other children her age was difficult. She could not smile, but she could vocalize laughter, which made her seem quite odd. Together with my German colleagues we transplanted a small muscle from her upper thigh and rewired some nerves. Not wanting to over-promise, I told her mother to expect some movement about six months after the surgery. The operation was a success and six weeks later she was smiling for the first time in her life. It was the shortest recovery of movement I have recorded so far.

The research and advances on facial nerve surgery continue. Today we are able to tap into the healthy nerve on the normal side of a face to send emotional instructions to the paralyzed side with what is called a cross-facial graft. Although this is my field and I understand how nerves work, I am still amazed every time I see a patient come back months after their surgery and their paralyzed face has begun to move.

It wasn't so long ago that common medical wisdom dictated that nerves cannot regenerate. But a year after I have performed one of these procedures and have to go back into the same area to do something else I can tell that the nerves I connected have grown. Nerves that started out as thin as a strand of hair will have tripled in size.

I enjoy nerve surgery although it is intense, time consuming, and intricate. But sometimes it is a simple concept that provides a solution to a face-deforming condition. For example, we are now working on moving tiny segments of muscles from the neck and brow and reconnecting them to the eyelids so they can help patients blink and protect their eyes after a stroke or facial paralysis.

Sometimes the solution to a surgical dilemma turns out to be as basic as push-pull mechanics. One Sunday morning I was driving to church when one of my residents at Johns Hopkins called to tell me they'd received a fifteen-year-old girl who'd been in a car accident. Above one of her eyes a blow had caused a significant dent in her forehead.

The surgeon on duty had looked at the x-rays and told the family that to fix it they would have to make a long incision across her scalp, fold down the facial tissue, and open her skull to push the bone back out, into place. My resident overheard and conferred with the staff surgeons about a different technique he had seen me perform.

He told the family, "There is an alternative to opening the skull and you should talk to this guy I work with because I'm pretty sure he can find a simpler way to fix this."

I made a U-turn and headed into Baltimore.

My resident had been right. The injury was not life-threatening but cutting her open as had been proposed would leave her with a big cosmetic problem—a long straight scar across her scalp or forehead—and a long recovery. Doing nothing would have left a prominent, disfiguring divot. I wanted to fix it without trading one cosmetic problem for another.

First, I made a tiny hole where the skull bone had caved

in. Then I inserted a thin tool with a hook on the end. Using a miniaturized camera to see what I was doing, I was able to pull the fractured bone back out where it belonged. Then, with another tool, I was able to squirt a special medical glue to hold everything in place. When it was all done and healed, the only evidence of the injury was a small spot that could just as easily have been an acne scar.

Those times when I can dramatically change the outcome for someone who would otherwise have had to go through a much more traumatic and complicated surgery are the greatest rewards of my career. So are times when someone I have trained and worked with uses that knowledge and skill to go the extra mile to dramatically alter the course of a life.

I was putting the finishing touches on my book one day when I got one of those calls worthy of a U-turn, except I was at home. Dr. Lisa E. Ishii, also an otolaryngologist and facial plastic surgeon, was on call when the Hopkins emergency room received a baby girl, not quite two years old, who had sustained a nightmarish injury.

A dog had nearly torn off half her chubby little face. The flesh was barely attached at one side and could be lifted like a book cover from the other. I love animals, but I have seen far too many cases of horrific facial wounds from dog attacks on small kids. For that reason, when our kids came along Adjoa and I decided we would not have a dog for a pet—one less thing to worry about.

This child's injury was so severe that nearly all the muscles and nerves that control the face were at risk of being severed. That was bad, but especially in so young a child: the nerves of infants are as thin as hair strands and difficult to identify, especially in the context of a catastrophic wound.

Without immediate microsurgery, while the wound was fresh and tissue easier to identify and work with, the child would surely grow up with a paralyzed face. In a community hospital that didn't happen to have the specialized equipment and experienced surgeons, the only option would be to reattach the facial flesh, sew her up, and pray for the best.

This little girl had the good fortune to end up in one of the only hospitals in our area that could save her smile. It would not be easy, so Dr. Ishii had called me to discuss the case. Even a battle-hardened surgeon cannot help reacting in a profoundly emotional way, and especially those who, like Dr. Ishii and myself, have been parents of young children.

"Kofi, I have to do everything I can for this kid."

I agreed, hung up, apologized to my children and my eternally patient Adjoa, and headed out the door for the one-hour drive to the hospital. All the way I was thinking through the options for how to put this little girl's face back together.

Leaving the highway ramp into Baltimore, I was dismayed to find the downtown streets near Hopkins had all been blocked for a marathon. With growing frustration, I drove around for three hours, mostly stuck in traffic, searching for a way through.

When I finally got to the operating room, Dr. Ishii was finishing up after nearly six solid hours of painstaking microsurgery, finding those filaments of nerve and tracing them, one by one, and reattaching severed muscles. She had put in a heroic and successful effort and given that child a second chance at a normal life.

That little girl will hopefully grow up remembering none of it. I'm sure that neither Dr. Ishii nor I will ever forget her.

CHAPTER 23:
A VERY IMPORTANT
MEETING

One Friday, in my seventh year on the faculty of Johns Hopkins University, I got home later than usual, dropped my bag in the hallway, and headed for the kitchen to have some dinner. When I sat down at the table in my usual seat, I found propped up in front of it a handwritten note in bold felt-tip colors in a child's script.

> *Daddy, It is very important that we meet tomorrow. Akua, Your Daughter.*

A pang of guilt tugged at my heart. Akua, who was eight at the time, had been trying to get my attention all week. Day after day, work interfered. She and the twin boys we'd had by then were accustomed to my frequent absences. It was the rare weeknight when I was there to pray with them at bedtime, as my parents did when I was their age.

When I'm not at Hopkins, I'm often traveling on medical missions, to conferences, or to other medical universities in other countries, studying and teaching the latest surgical techniques.

At Hopkins I've got a reputation for being a Dr. Yes— someone who, if asked to pitch in with a difficult case, cannot say "No." Thus both my clinical and academic duties keep me constantly busy. Each morning I leave home at six o'clock for the one-hour drive to work. On a "slow" day I'll pull into the driveway about nine at night.

As I ate I speculated. What was on Akua's mind? Perhaps it was the trip to Disneyland she had been lobbying for, or a new children's movie she wanted to watch. Or (a parent's imagination will tend to roam), perhaps someone at her school, where she was one of very few black children, had made a hurtful comment about her hair or the color of her skin.

Each day that week I had promised to come home early that night and we would have a "meeting," as she so charmingly put it. If your daddy is always saying he has to go to a meeting, one way to get his attention is to give him a meeting he has to go to.

Each day, circumstances conspired against me—a trauma case that came in late needing urgent attention; an afternoon surgery delayed for hours; a procedure that proved unexpectedly challenging and time consuming.

As I reflected, I realized that there was always something unexpected. If it wasn't direct patient care it was an academic obligation or any of the ever-growing list of things doctors have to do these days to practice medicine: battles with electronic records systems; letters to insurance companies; patient phone calls and emails to return; papers to write and publishing deadlines.

The weeks were flying by and began extending into the weekends as well. I was missing too many of my kids' sports events and music recitals.

The next morning I woke up determined to honor Akua's request. She, uncharacteristically, had gotten up early. She came downstairs with her face set in an expression of sober determination. We sat down on the sofa and she dove right in.

"Daddy, why is it that you have no time for me but lots of time for other people?"

She'd caught me completely off guard. I paused to think about how to explain, as I had before, that Daddy is helping other people who are not as lucky as she when—on cue—my ever-present phone rang where it was sitting on the cushion, symbolically between us. Akua knew that calls at such an hour on a Saturday morning could only be from the hospital, and that it would be something urgent.

Before I could reach to answer she had snatched the phone off the sofa cushion. Her forehead furrowed with exasperation she stabbed the answer button and declared in a loud, clear voice, "Dr. Boahene is not available. He is taking care of another very important patient—his daughter!"

Then, with a sigh of resignation, she handed the phone to me. A patient was indeed in crisis and I had to rush off to perform an emergency procedure. My heart ached on that morning's drive to Baltimore. Without my noticing, I had fallen victim to a syndrome common among surgeons—my work/life balance was off kilter.

For one thing, my subspecialty, skull base surgery, is a busy discipline and it's growing. Meanwhile, there has been a substantial decline in interest among American medical students in pursuing surgical careers. State by state surveys report "substantial" shortages in a number of subspecialities. Surgery has evolved so much, thanks to technology, that students need to know more than ever.

Beside those external factors, I was caught in the cycle of just being too busy to figure out how to be less busy. I realized that I could not remember the last time I had a dream. When you are too busy you forget to dream, forget to invest in your health, forget the priority of family life.

It has been four years since my "very important meeting" with eight-year-old Akua and I am still exploring how to balance work with my family life. For some surgeons, it's a choice rather than a balance. A prominent neurosurgeon I know—whose patients had included a couple of US presidents and was at the peak of his career—showed up at work one day and announced he was retiring to focus on his family life. It shocked everyone, and made me think.

On my twins' tenth birthday, Jonathan said, "Dad, you better pay attention. Kids these days grow up fast!" I don't know where he heard that, but coming from him it left a strong impression.

One my residency mates at Mayo, Dr. Holger Gassner, had once said, "Kofi, I'm worried about you." He thought I might be stuck in a mindset that can lead to burnout or a health crisis. I recalled his warning when a I found myself facing a health issue that threatened my entire career.

It began one day about three years ago after a short morning surgery. A surgical assistant looked at me cockeyed, squinted, and asked, "What happened to your eye?"

I hadn't felt anything and my vision had been fine. When I

took off my protective glasses and looked in a mirror I could see that my right eye was a little swollen. My guess was that some contaminant had splashed on me during the surgery. I washed the eye and then dressed for afternoon clinic.

That night I began to feel a slight pain in the eye and the swelling had gotten worse. I applied lubricating ointment and went to bed.

The next morning the eye was throbbing and even more swollen. Within hours I was at the hospital with several colleague-specialists looking down at me with their furrowed brows, putting me through a battery of tests. Their care and concern was both reassuring and scary. Meanwhile, the vision in the affected eye was becoming blurred.

When a member of my family, including myself, becomes ill, I mentally run through the list of possible worst-case diagnoses. For the first time in my career my work came screeching to a halt. My sight, like my hands, is essential. I work in the 3-D world of tiny camera lenses, lights, and tools that can snoop around and fix things under the brain without disturbing the brain. Two sharp eyes are required. Had my career come to an abrupt end? Or worse, was my life on the line?

What would I say to my family? My children—had I prepared them well for life? How would I break the news? What would I do if I could no longer be a surgeon?

My eye was so swollen when I got home that night that there was no hiding it from the kids. I gathered them together with Adjoa and told them what was happening.

When I finished, James, the older of my twin boys (by five minutes), said in a confident tone, "Dad, it seems like this is one of those times that your children should hold your hands and pray for you. Everything will be all right."

That's a moment I cherish, when I knew beyond all doubt that my children would be fine no matter what happened to me.

James turned out to be right. We did hold hands and pray. The following week my ophthalmology colleagues assured me that my problem was an inflammation treatable with antibiotics. Within a week or so, I was able to return to the microscope, threading sutures finer than a human hair. With my restored vision also came personal clarity.

Today my work/life balancing includes involving my children in my overseas work. Like my father, I want to raise missionaries. I also want to encourage in them a true appreciation for the advantages and privileges they have had.

So, on a recent surgical mission to Ghana, I took twelve-year-old Akua with me. We had a lot of time to talk and just be together on the plane trips, just the two of us. In Ghana she got to know her grandparents on a deeper level (and see where they sleep!), meet some aunts, uncles, and cousins, and get to know the source of her stream in a way she's likely to remember as a highlight of her childhood.

When it was time for me to go to work, I prepared my first young patients for surgery while Akua sat in the children's ward with her iPad, entertaining the rest of the kids, reading aloud, and telling stories. My heart overflowed with tenderness to see her taking the first steps in her journey, following the paths of both her father and grandfather.

CHAPTER 24:
MOSQUITOES AND
OTHER SMALL THINGS

During one of my recent medical missions to Rwanda I had a profound, small-world experience that left me feeling both gratified and humbled. It happened when someone I'd never met recognized my face.

In my scrubs, mask pulled down, I was waiting in a hallway for my next patient to finish receiving a pre-operation blood transfusion. I was thinking about the procedure when I noticed a young man in his twenties lingering awkwardly nearby. My attention seemed to startle him and he stalked off, head down, stealing a sideways glance at me as he passed.

A short while later he appeared again, this time with another young man with whom he conferred for a moment and then pointed toward me. Wearing nervous grins, they approached like a couple of shy but eager puppies.

The first one gazed at me with wide eyes. "I-I was just telling my friend, 'That's Dr. Boahene.' But he didn't believe me. 'No way,' he said. But I was sure of it. We know about you. We're medical students and we've read about you. We saw you on CNN. You're our hero."

I burst out laughing. Somehow, without my noticing, my story had made its way back to Africa and spread. In the States I was just another doctor from Africa, a nobody in a society full of notables. Although I had been filmed for a CNN segment on its *African Voices* program, it was intended for broadcast in Africa and got little attention in the US. It was delightful to be recognized back home.

I gave the students a few encouraging words before I was called to begin the next operation. It put me in such a good mood to know that my journey was inspiring others to follow. It was also a humbling reminder of all the Samaritans who helped make that journey possible, and of how much work needs to be done before future generations of African medical students will no longer have to depend on lucky breaks, divine interventions, and the kindness of strangers.

Until that time, for every uplifting story about the work of medical missionaries there are many times that number of heart-breaking examples of suffering for lack of the most basic care and medical supplies. This I know from observation but especially from personal experience.

A dear uncle of mine spent weeks in pain for lack of a medical device as familiar to Americans as a Band-Aid. A beloved aunt died after a misdiagnosis so basic an experienced frequent flyer could have guessed it. These are things that keep me up at night.

After performing a complex procedure in a state-of-the-art operating theater at one of the world's best hospitals, I sometimes drive home into the prosperous, rolling farmland of the Maryland suburbs feeling the weight of that dichotomy. Although great strides have been made in fighting infectious diseases like malaria, AIDS, and Ebola, pills and injections can't diagnose a disease or set a broken bone or mend a lip or remove a tumor.

All the medical missions on Earth can't fix the underlying problem—the developing world needs to nurture its own internists, diagnosticians, anesthesiologists, surgeons, and nurses and to provide access to professional facilities and equipment. For this reason, my top goal now is to raise the funds to build a specialty surgical hospital in Ghana. It will be a place where young African men and women can receive specialized surgical training with which they will be able to make a living providing world-class surgical care to their fellow Ghanaians and West Africans.

I am convinced that an approach that trains specialists locally in Africa is the most effective way of transferring and building expertise with the least pressure of brain drain. Towards this goal, in 2014 I established a non-profit organization, Foundation for Special Surgery (FSS), whose main mission is to provide the highest level of sub-specialized surgical care to patients in sub-Saharan Africa. The vision of the foundation is to become a leader in training the next generation of sub-specialized surgeons in the region by enlisting the participation of world-class surgeons from the US, Europe, Africa, Latin America, and Asia.

This is a big vision but I have proof of concept in the

story of the Mayo family. Over the years all but one of my siblings have emigrated to the US and ended up with careers in medicine or a health-related field. There is a pharmacy manager, an anesthesiologist, an otolaryngologist/facial plastics surgeon, a nurse specialist, a medical technologist, and a health informatics software engineer.

Our success is a testament to my parent's sacrifices, prayers, and encouragement. We share a vision of giving back to the source of our streams, but as with the Mayos, it will take more than one family to build a lasting institution with substantial impact. Across the globe, I have shared my vision with my mentors, colleagues, former residents, and friends in the medical field and there has been no shortage of volunteers who are eager to transfer their expertise.

For now, care in certain places in Africa can be so shockingly primitive that even the best efforts we make as missionaries can't compensate. A tragic example was a boy who developed an infection after we repaired his palate. The child became so ill he needed to be put on a respirator, but the only available equipment was a bag valve mask, a manual device that is typically used by first responders at an accident scene.

For two entire days, members of our team took turns sitting next to this boy and manually pumping oxygen into his lungs while someone tried to find a mechanical respirator that would do the job automatically. Our team's departure time arrived to return to the States but no mechanical respirator could be found.

With heavy hearts we had no choice but to leave that child in the care of the locals. As we feared might happen, he died a week or so later.

While on a non-mission visit home, a relative alerted me to the suffering of a dear old uncle, a man who had once been a high-level finance official in the government, someone who one might expect to have access to the best care. He had been in increasing discomfort for weeks due to an enlarged prostate that was making it impossible for him to empty his bladder. Were he in the US he would have had ready access to a catheter—a simple, inexpensive tube device that is inserted through the ureter into the bladder sack. Catheters are relatively cheap and in much of the developed world can be bought by consumers online.

I went to see him at his home and a quick exam confirmed his bladder was full. No one had attempted to find him a catheter and, furthermore, it appeared none were to be had at the local hospital. I'm sensitive to the feelings of health-care workers in places like Ghana, so I try not to step on toes or say anything that would appear condescending or demanding. But the situation was headed toward a crisis and the patient was a close relative. I ran around the city from hospital to hospital looking for the right-sized catheter. With some persistence, and pulling rank, I was able to get a hospital worker to scrounge one up.

After a local doctor tried and failed to pass this new catheter, at my suggestion he successfully inserted a needle through my uncle's belly into his bladder. With the needle inserted, I was able to drain about 60 ounces of urine from an organ with a normal capacity of about 12 to 20. The pain had been excruciating, unnecessary, and, in an elderly man, could have led to a fatal systemic infection.

Experiences like that are frustrating and have made me

hyper-aware of how much we here in the States take for granted that the best medical care and supplies are just a phone call away. Waste is a particular pet peeve and that has earned me a reputation for what others have called my mother-isms. One of my mother-isms involves the use of common surgical supplies like sutures. The needle and thread that surgeons use comes in individual packages and a typical procedure will require a number of these packages to close a wound or incision.

In most any hospital, operating room nurses who are preparing for a procedure will open as many suture packages in advance as they estimate will be needed. It's a convenience but inevitably there are some left over that have to be discarded because they are no longer sterile. In a large, well-financed place like Hopkins it's easy to forget that a little waste here and there adds up. Knowing how hard it was to find a simple catheter in Ghana, any waste feels unconscionable to me. So when I'm operating, I instruct the support staff not to open the suture packages until I know I'll need them. Some may think it's petty, but I want to stay true to my beliefs and set a good example.

One of the most personally disheartening experiences involved an aunt I loved deeply. She lived in the town where I went to boarding school and I spent many hours with her during school breaks and on weekends. A seamstress, she taught me how to sew and I helped her make dresses that she sold in the market. I knew in those days I wanted to be a doctor but it was a fortuitous coincidence that I learned how to work a needle and thread at a young age. Like creating my own toys, it was another experience that prepared me for what I do now.

The last time I saw my aunt was on a visit home. Two weeks later, I learned that she had died from a blood clot. She had gone to see a doctor complaining of pain in one of her legs after a long bus ride. Without a test to confirm she had it she was prescribed medicine for malaria and told that was the cause of her discomfort. A second doctor diagnosed her pain as arthritis of the hip and recommended surgery.

Instead, the pain she felt was a deep vein thrombosis in her leg, the kind of blood clot that can develop from sitting too long (as on an airplane or bus) and can occasionally break free, travel through the bloodstream, and become lodged in the lungs. This is known as a pulmonary embolism and may cause chest pain, shortness of breath, and, in severe cases, sudden death. It was a terrible loss and a great frustration knowing her death might have been prevented.

This problem has deep, stubborn roots. Patients in the developed world enjoy discussing the details of their conditions with their doctors, have access to the latest information via the Internet, and are unafraid to seek second opinions. Patients sometimes show up in my office with binders full of material they have accumulated about their particular condition and my relationship with them is collaborative.

In African and similar post-colonial cultures, doctors are revered and stand at the top of the social hierarchy. That discourages dialogue between doctor and patient. Whatever the doctor says is gospel.

Another factor is that malaria has a broad range of symptoms and is so prevalent in West Africa that a third or more of the regional population—128 million people—has it at any given time, according to a 2014 World Health

Organization report. Overburdened doctors see so much of it that it's tempting to go with what they know. This is especially true when equipment and other diagnostic basics are scarce.

Patients in poorer nations are reluctant to see a doctor without a compelling reason and they often can't afford the fees for private practitioners. When they do get in to see a doctor they are deferential and the exchange is one-sided. Interactions I have with Africans versus Americans are starkly different.

An American doctor might find an African patient reluctant, taciturn, and uncertain. Africans aren't used to the standard history-taking that is automatic in the US and elsewhere. Patients struggle with how to answer the questions. My missionary colleagues might say, "They don't know what they are here for."

The cultural norm in such societies is to tell the doctor what's wrong, "My leg hurts," and expect the doctor to automatically know what to do. When he or she doesn't, the patient is likely to be sent home with a package of malaria medication.

The point of all these stories is not to bemoan the unnecessary waste of life or to criticize a broken system of care. The main idea I hope readers will take away from these examples and the many twists and turns in my journey is that small acts often have big consequences.

An otherwise insignificant interaction with a visa clerk in Moscow made it possible for me to come to America. A small act of kindness by an Arkansas ex-convict turned a potentially terrifying ordeal on a dark night into a moment of redemption and a renewal of faith. An overheard snippet of conversation in a US consulate in Mexico made it possible for me to continue my work at Mayo. An alert doctor took just seconds to completely change the life of a teenager who was assumed to be mentally deficient but was simply tongue-tied.

After I left the Mayo clinic, I got a letter from the development office informing me that a patient had donated an anonymous gift to the clinic in my honor for the care they received from me. Looking back, I cannot recall anything particularly special that I did for that patient. It must have been one of those small acts.

I have witnessed and benefitted from many small acts of kindness and whenever possible I try to publicly acknowledge them. I have often spoken about the late Jerry Manion, my professor at the University of Central Arkansas who, on good faith alone, made possible my medical education simply by scrawling his signature on a piece of paper.

The school recently honored me as its Alumni of the Year and I returned to Conway to accept it. With Jerry Manion's widow and children in the audience, along with my American mother, Cindy Lennon, and her family, I told the story of how Jerry came to be my salvation, and about the profound gratitude of a father who was able to see his son smile properly for the first time.

It gave me such pleasure to be able to spread the word, possibly inspire others to follow the examples set by Jerry and the Lennons, and to invoke another favorite African proverb, sometimes attributed to the Dalai Lama, to illustrate the point: If you think you are too small to make a difference, try sleeping in a closed room with a mosquito.

ADINKRA ICONS GUIDE*

Nyame Ye Ohene

[Nía-Mih Yeh, Oh-He-Nih]

Translation
God is King

Symbolism
Omnipresence

Epa

[Eh-Pah]

Translation
Handcuffs

Symbolism
Justice

Funtummireku Denkyemmireku

[Foh-N-Too-Mih-Rey-Koo Den-Chem-Mih-Rey-Koo]

Translation
Siamese Crocodiles - Stomach Joined

Symbolism
Democracy

Akoko Nan

[Ah-Koh-Koh Nan]

Translation
Hen's Feet

Symbolism
Parenthood

Osram Ne Nsoroma

[Aw-Sram Nih N-Soh-Roh-mah]

Translation
The Moon and Star

Symbolism
Fondness

Mframadan

[M-Fra-Mah-Dan]

Translation
Wind Proof House

Symbolism
Fortitude

Hwemudua

[Sh-Weh-Moo-Duah]

Translation
Measuring Rod

Symbolism
Excellence

Okodee Mmowere

[Aw-Koh-Deeh Moh-We-Reh]

Translation
Eagle's Talons

Symbolism
Strength and Unity

Ntesie Mate Masie

[N-Teh-Sih-Eh Mah-Tih Mah-Sih-Eh]

Translation
I've Heard and Kept It

Symbolism
Knowledge and Wisdom

Gyawu Atiko

[Jay-Woo Ay-Tih-Koh]

Translation
Symbol for Chief Gyawu

Symbolism
Fearlessness

Nyami Nti

[Nía-Mih N-Ti]

Translation
By God's Grace

Symbolism
Faith and Grace

Dono

[Doh-Noh]

Translation
Bell Drum

Symbolism
Praise

* Source: The Noun Project / NCOC Ghana / Wikipedia
http://adinkraproject.com/

Akofena

[Ah-Koh-Fina]

Translation
Royal Sword

Symbolism
Valor

Nea Ope Se Obedi Hene

[Niya Opah Seh Oh-Bedi Hh-Nih]

Translation
He who wants to be King

Symbolism
Leadership

Nyame Dua

[Nia-Mih Duah]

Translation
Tree of God

Symbolism
Divine Presence

Ese Ne Tekrema

[Eh-Sih Nih Tak-Reh-Mah]

Translation
Teeth and Tongue

Symbolism
Interdependence

Nsoromma

[N-Soh-Rah-Mah]

Translation
Child of The Heavens

Symbolism
Guardianship

Fofoo

[Fah-Fuh]

Translation
Fofoo Plant - Yellow Flowered Plant

Symbolism
Jealousy

Akoben

[Ah-Koh-Ben]

Translation
War Horn

Symbolism
Vigilance

Fawohudie

[Fah-Woh-Hoo-Dieh]

Translation
Freedom

Symbolism
Freedom

Dame Dame

[Dah-Mih Dah-Mih]

Translation
Board Game

Symbolism
Intelligence

Hye Wo Nhye

[Shih-Woh-N-Shih]

Translation
Cannot Be Burnt

Symbolism
Infinite

Akoma

[Ah-Koh-Ma]

Translation
The Heart

Symbolism
Love

Pempamsie

[Peh-M-Pah-M-Sih-Eh]

Translation
Readiness

Symbolism
Readiness

Mmere Dane

[Mih-Reh Dah-Nih]

Translation
Times Changes

Symbolism
Change

Eban

[Eh-ban]

Translation
Fence

Symbolism
Protection

Asase Ye Duru

[Ah-Sah-Sih Yeh Dru]

Translation
The Earth is Heavy

Symbolism
Providence

Sankofa: Alternate

[Sah-N-Koh-Fah]

Translation
Return and get it

Symbolism
Learn from the past

Kuntinkantan

[Koh-N-Tin-Koh-N-Tan]

Translation
Don't Boast or Be Proud

Symbolism
Humility

Bese Saka

[Bih-Sih Sah-Kah]

Translation
Sack of Cola Nuts

Symbolism
Affluence

Sesa Woruban

[Seh-Sah Woh-Roo-ban]

Translation
Change Your Life

Symbolism
Transformation

Ananse Ntontan

[Ah-Nan-Sih N-Ton-Tan]

Translation
Spider Web

Symbolism
Creativity

Owuo Atwedee

[O-Wuo Ah-Chweh-Deh]

Translation
Ladder of Death

Symbolism
Fate

Wawa Aba

[Wah-Wah Ah-Bah]

Translation
Wawa Tree Seed

Symbolism
Skillfulness

Aya

[Ah-Yah]

Translation
Fern

Symbolism
Endurance

Nkyinkyim

[N-Chin-N-Chim]

Translation:
Twisting

Symbolism
Dynamism

Odo Nyera Fie Kwan

[O-Don Nie-Ra Fi-Eh Kwa-N]

Translation
Love does not lose its way home

Symbolism
Faithfulness

Kete Pa

[Keh-Teh Pah]

Translation
Good Mat

Symbolism
Love and Faithfulness

Tamfo Bebre

[Tah-M-Foh Beh-Breh]

Translation
The Enemy Shall Suffer

Symbolism
Envy

Odenkyem

[O-Den-Chim]

Translation
The Crocodile

Symbolism
Prudence

Bi Nnka Bi

[Bih-N-Kah Bih]

Translation
Don't Bite Others

Symbolism
Peace

Me Ware Wo

[Meh Wah-Reh Woh]

Translation
I'll Marry You

Symbolism
Commitment

Gye Nyame

[Jih-N-Yeh-Nih]

Translation
Except God

Symbolism
Omnipotence

Akoma Ntoaso

[Ah-Koh-Ma N-Toh-Aso]

Translation
United Hearts

Symbolism
Understanding

Nea Onnim No Sua A Ohu

[Niya Oh-Nim Nah Sua A Ohoo]

Translation
He who does not know can know from Learning

Symbolism
Learning

Owo Foro Adobe

[Aw-Woh Poh-Roh Ah-Doh-Beh]

Translation
Snake climbing a palm tree

Symbolism
Against All Odds

Nssa

[N-Sah]

Translation
Woven Fabric

Symbolism
Authenticity

Wuforo Dua Pa A

[Woo-Poh-Roh Du-Ah Pah Ah]

Translation
When You Climb A Good Tree

Symbolism
Support and Encouragement

Mpatapo

[M-Pah-Tah-Poh]

Translation
Reconciliation Knot

Symbolism
Reconciliation

Nyansapo

[Nia-N-San-Poh]

Translation
Wisdom Knot

Symbolism
Wisdom

Mpuannum

[M-Puh-Ah-Noom]

Translation
Five Tufts of Hair

Symbolism
Loyalty

Krapa

[Krah-Pah]

Translation
Pure Heart

Symbolism
Purity

Boa Me Na Me Boa Wo

[Boa Mih Nah Mih Boa Woh]

Translation
Help Me to Help You

Symbolism
Cooperation

Nkonsonkonson

[N-Kon-Son-N-Kon-Son]

Translation
Chain Links

Symbolism
Human Relations

Fihankra

[Fih-Han-Krak]

Translation
Compound House

Symbolism
Security

Adinkrahene

[Ad-In-Kra-Haney]

Translation
Adinkra King

Symbolism
Greatness

Wo Nsa Da Mu A

[Woh N-Sah Duh Moo Ah]

Translation
If Your Hands Are In The Dish

Symbolism
Pluralism

Onyankopon Adom

[O-Nu-N-Koh-Pun Ah-Dom]

Translation
God's Grace

Symbolism
Hope and Faith

Duafe

[Dush-Fih]

Translation
Wooden Comb

Symbolism
Femininity

Nhwimu

[N-Shui-Moo]

Translation
Crossed Divisions on Cloth

Symbolism
Precision

Dwannimmen

[Jwah-Nih-Men]

Translation
Horns of a Ram

Symbolism
Humility and Strength

Sankofa

[Sah-N-Koh-Fah]

Translation
Return and get it

Symbolism
Learn from the past

Nyame Nnwu Na Me Wu

[Naa-Mih-N-Woo Nah Meh Woo]

Translation
God Never Dies; So I Won't Die

Symbolism
Afterlife

Biribi Wo Soro

[Bih-Rih-Bih Woh Soh-Roh]

Translation
Something Exists Up There

Symbolism
Hope

34482408R00163

Made in the USA
Middletown, DE
25 August 2016